The Function of Theory
in Composition Studies

The Function of Theory
in Composition Studies

Raúl Sánchez

State University of New York Press

Published by
State University of New York Press, Albany

For information, address State University of New York Press, 194 Washington Avenue, Suite 305, Albany, NY 12210-2365

Production by Stephanie M. Deyette
Marketing by Anne M. Valentine

Library of Congress Cataloging-in-Publication Data

Sanchez, Raul, 1965–
    The function of theory in composition studies / Raul Sanchez.
      p. cm.
    Includes bibliographical references and index.
    ISBN 0-7914-6477-6 (alk. paper)
    1. English language—Composition and exercises—Study and teaching.
2. English language—Rhetoric—Study and teaching. 3. Report writing—Study and teaching. I. Title.

PE1401.S325 2005
808'.042'071—dc22   2004057867

10 9 8 7 6 5 4 3 2 1

for my family

Contents

Acknowledgments

There are many to thank, but I begin with my colleagues in the University Writing Program and the Department of English at the University of Utah. Their support and encouragement have helped me see this project to completion:

First among them is Susan Miller, whose work serves as a foundation and point of departure for this project's argument, whose enduring theoretical and historical interest in the act of writing has profoundly influenced my approach to composition studies, and whose mentoring during my time in Utah has made me a better writer and teacher.

Thanks also to Howard Horwitz, who read this work in its various stages of development, always with a generous combination of enthusiasm and constructive criticism.

And thanks to the program directors and department chairs who have provided time and contexts in which I was able to write: John Ackerman, Michael Rudick, Tom Huckin, Maureen Mathison, Stephen Tatum, Charles Berger, and Stuart Culver.

Beyond Utah, more thanks are due:

To Gary Olson, who taught me half of what I know, who helped get this project off the ground, and who has always supported it, despite disagreeing with "almost every single word."

To Victor Villanueva. What this project owes to him may not be evident, but the debt is real and deep, just the same. He knows what I mean.

To my colleagues and friends in the Latino Caucus of NCTE, whose very presence serves always to remind me of the contexts in which I write and the goals to which I'm committed.

To Sid Dobrin, Julie Drew, and Joe Hardin, who cheerfully endure the rambling and often intemperate e-mails in which I try to work through pesky theoretical problems and who, with equal cheer, let me know when I am writing nonsense.

And finally, to Priscilla Ross and SUNY Press, for helping to improve and agreeing to publish, this book.

✢ 1 ✢

The Current State
of Composition Theory

The function of theory in composition studies is to provide generalized accounts of what writing is and how it works. These accounts can both guide and derive from the results of empirical research and, in the case of student writing, from classroom practice. Contrary to the beliefs of some composition theorists, it is possible and, more importantly, necessary for composition studies to have an agenda for inquiry comprised of theory and empirical research in a mutually informing relationship. What is required is for all involved to acknowledge the necessarily contingent nature of both theory and empirical research. As Carol Berkenkotter pointed out long ago, the argument against empiricism is more appropriately directed at positivism, and as such it is one with which many empirical researchers in composition studies would agree (70). Once we, as theorists and researchers, have dispensed with any residual legacies of positivism, we should be able to proceed in good faith with the business of the field: to study writing by methodically observing and analyzing the many and varied instances of it (i.e., empirical research) and by making warranted, general, and possibly predictive statements about it (i.e., theory).

Of course, I have just described an ideal world of neatly drawn and readily agreed-upon categories. The real world of

1

scholarly inquiry is more complicated, more contested, and considerably more interesting than is the platonic scene depicted above. In composition studies, the boundary between those activities called "empirical research" and "theory" is on occasion breached, and to good effect. For example, an empirical researcher such as Linda Flower generalizes her findings in light of theory, and she explicitly frames her research according to theoretical formulations. Likewise, a theorist such as Susan Miller has brought considerable theoretical insight to bear on archival material.[1]

But such examples of our field's potential for methodological richness and theoretical variety are exceptions rather than the rule. For some time, composition theory has been largely irrelevant to empirical research, and vice versa. The two seem to have little to do with each other. When empiricists need theory with which to ground their research, they seem to go elsewhere, lately to activity theory and other work outside of composition studies. Likewise, practitioners of composition theory often take it for granted that their colleagues' empirical research has little to offer them, so they do not even read it. This split may be long-standing, but I believe it deepened in the late 1980s and early 1990s, when composition theory began to develop as an independent discourse.

As its title indicates, this book is about composition theory: its condition and prospects. It is an extended analysis of the consequences of a dominant theoretical disposition in the field, which I will begin to discuss below. It is also an argument for a different theoretical disposition. Of course, I hope that my argument will persuade composition theorists to think differently about their work than they currently might. And I hope it will allow composition theory and empirical research to interact more fully. Finally, I am interested in making it possible for composition theory to offer better descriptions of writing, accounts that better match the textual realities many people experience today, realities that increasingly outmoded adjectives such as "modern" and "postmodern" no longer capture. Toward these ends, then, this book makes a somewhat ironic argument: namely, that the period of composition theory's ascendance coincides with its having stopped making trenchant theoretical statements about writing. The proliferation of composition theory, beginning in the early 1990s, was marked primarily by articles and books that applied existing theories from outside of composition studies to issues in composition studies, but it did not offer many genuinely new theoretical perspectives on writing.

Throughout this book, I will show how a very familiar and now inaccurate model of writing has persisted doggedly in composition theory despite the boom of the 1990s, despite the significant increase in the amount and variety of theoretical discourse in the field. I examine some key concepts that have informed composition theory since that time, showing how and why they did not result in different theories of writing. And, in a theoretical departure from the implicit premises of that work, I identify *theory* as a function of writing. In terms of our usual categories for thinking about theoretical issues, I consider my approach to writing and to theory itself to be neither essentialist nor anti-essentialist, neither modern nor postmodern. Such categories occupy the terrain of hermeneutics. And hermeneutics, I will argue, poses a major obstacle to the study of writing. In fact, a dependence on hermeneutics and its corollary, representation, characterizes the composition theory I wish to examine. This dependence limits composition theory's ability to describe the function and nature of writing in an increasingly networked world. In this world, the most striking features of writing are its sheer proliferation and its constant, rapid circulation. Neither hermeneutics nor a paradigm of representation is capable of recognizing, much less describing, the implications for writing of such an environment. In fact, this thoroughly ingrained hermeneutic disposition limits composition theory's ability to characterize writing as anything more than a technology of representation, a means by which to either transmit or generate that which is considered noumenal, abstract, or conceptual. In the chapters that follow, I will show how this disposition manifests in the field's understanding of writing's relationship to concepts of *knowledge, ideology,* and *culture,* each of which has, in different ways, played formative roles in the development of composition theory since the late 1980s and early 1990s. Along the way, and then explicitly in the final chapter, I will argue that composition theory can break with the hermeneutic disposition and the paradigm of representation by acknowledging that traditional, conceptual tools for thinking about writing are instead products and functions of writing. This revisionist theory will also have the added benefit, I hope, of helping develop future empirical research, thus bringing into productive dialogue the two major branches of inquiry in composition studies.

The Problem of Hermeneutics

In the simplest terms, we can describe the hermeneutic disposition as the steadfast and persistent belief in a consequential difference between words and things. In composition studies, most theoretical work subscribes to this belief and, in turn, to the assumption that writing's most salient feature is its ability to represent *something else,* something that is not itself related fundamentally to writing or language. In contrast, I take representation neither as writing's signature function, nor as an ontological given (as literary studies seems to do), but as a structural component within a general system of discursive circulation and dissemination. From this perspective, the function of composition studies, and of composition theory in particular, is to describe and explain all features of that general system. Such a mandate would compel composition theory to reaffirm writing as its object of study, and to reject a narrow emphasis on representation as the conceptual and analytical core of its project. In other words, the function of theory in composition studies would be to attend to more than just the politics of representation.

This reaffirmation of writing is necessary due to the current state of composition theory. In the place of writing, concepts such as knowledge, ideology, and culture have claimed composition theory's attention as scholars have tried to explain how they appear to work through discourse. But it is a crucial theoretical mistake to assume that such concepts are fundamentally distinct from writing, that words and things are basically distinct even when closely intertwined. In doing so, we inadvertently take up familiar Platonic and Cartesian perspectives rather than generating perspectives that would be more appropriate to the conditions of Western civilization in the twenty-first century. As a result, composition theory is currently unable to account for the force and function of writing in a world that bears little relation to the one fantasized by hermeneutic theorists of the twentieth century, such as Hans Georg Gadamer, from whom so much of the current hermeneutic disposition is derived.

This chapter in particular attends to the "writtenness" of theory in order to frame the specific examinations undertaken elsewhere in the book. In claiming that knowledge, ideology, and culture are best considered not as ontological or epistemological concepts but as effects or products of writing, I am trying to make two points. First, I am offering a critique of certain theoretical assumptions about key terms in composition theory. Second and simultaneously, I am arguing for a different approach to writing—to the act or phenomenon of writing—than composition theory has put forth to date. By identifying *as* writing the theoretical apparatus brought to bear *on* writing, I hope not only to revise the particular components of that apparatus but also to re-envision the enterprise of composition theory. I want to propose a different theoretical practice, one predicated on a different, non-hermeneutic description writing. That is, I want to propose another disposition, a different way of writing and otherwise operating theoretically.

So, while the book as a whole proposes a different theoretical disposition toward writing, this chapter in particular urges a new approach to theory. Rearticulating both will require a good deal more than the familiar admission that most human activity requires or takes place through or in written or otherwise

signifying discourse. It will require more than a newly invigo-
rated Writing Across the Curriculum theory, or any other theory
that understands writing as either a medium or generator of
something else that, in the end, is not the same as writing. For
example, it will require the rejection of the belief that writing
shapes thought in favor of the understanding that *thought* is itself
a term, usually honorific, attached retrospectively to always-
already-written texts: a term that, in turn, directs present and
future uses and transformations (themselves always written) of
these texts. In other words, describing writing in the way I am
proposing will require composition theory to commit itself to
textuality more thoroughly than it has in the recent past. It will
require us to relentlessly and scrupulously bracket all *ideas*, to
place in quotation marks (or italics) every deeply seated and
casually assumed *concept*, even those around which composition
studies has formed its intellectual and professional identity, such
as *rhetoric* and *the subject*, which will be the topics of chapter
5, while chapters 2, 3, and 4 will address in detail knowledge,
ideology, and culture, respectively. Each will be subjected to
what I will call grammatological scrutiny.

Grammatology and Writing

My interest in reformulating composition theory around a non-
hermeneutic description of writing draws heavily on Derrida's
earlier writings. Some might consider this work to be dated. After
all, it is by now common to suppose that the lessons of what is
called deconstruction have been thoroughly learned and even
internalized by English studies and in the hermeneutically dis-
posed quarters of composition theory. Scholars and theorists
frequently claim to have "deconstructed" this or that concept,
which act usually amounts, however, to some traditional form of
ideological or philosophical critique. What passes for
deconstruction is often little more than the familiar modernist

tactic of debunking or demystifying. In this way, deconstruction has been assimilated and domesticated into composition studies. Derrida's early texts claim that writing is a paradigmatic human activity.[2] As he notes in *Of Grammatology*, writing "designate[s] not only the physical gestures of literal pictographic or ideographic inscription, but also the totality of what makes it possible; and also, beyond the signifying face, the signified face itself" (9). A grammatological approach to writing proposes that writing itself underlies all the conceptual, theoretical, philosophical, and even rhetorical activity habitually brought to bear on writing, as well as on terms such as *language* and *discourse*. It argues that concepts in which composition theorists regularly traffic—*knowledge, ideology, culture,* and also *rhetoric* and *the subject*—are best approached not as concepts at all but as examples of, enactments of, writing.

One could, of course, argue that the force of Derrida's argument is diminished by the fact that he differentiates between two kinds of writing. On the one hand there is "arche-writing," an abstract (i.e., "non-empirical," to use his term) concept that sets in motion the very mechanisms of signification. It is, according to Derrida, "that very thing which cannot let itself be reduced to the form of presence" (57). On the other hand there is "the vulgar concept of writing," or "writing in the narrow sense," which derives from speech and is a product or function of logocentrism (56). According to Derrida, through acts of "historical repression" the vulgar or narrow form of writing has stood in for arche-writing, has been presented as the only possible kind of writing in order to conceal the writtenness of human activity (56). Thus, one could argue, arche-writing is not really writing, as people in composition studies understand it.

Furthermore, one could argue that Derrida's differentiation between arche-writing and narrow writing limits his work's usefulness for composition studies precisely because our field works with the latter rather than the former, which Derrida himself claims "cannot and can never be recognized as the object of a science" (57). Or, one might take the opposite stance and claim that arche-writing, rather than narrow writing, is precisely the main thing to which composition studies should attend, that this catalyst of signification is the rightful province of a field that means to point out the writtenness of and in the world.

Each of these arguments rests on the assumption that the difference between the abstract "arche-writing" and the empirical, "narrow writing" in Derrida's text is rigid and absolute. To be sure, Derrida's theory requires the nonempirical "arche-writing" because it views empiricism suspiciously as a feature of phonocentrism and logocentrism. It sees the subject-object relationship required by and for empiricism as not being an ontological given, as not comprising the natural order of things. "Arche-writing," or writing-in-general, is completely abstract, and because of this, postmodern composition theorists might focus on it at the expense of the empirical version of writing, thus moving away from considerations of the temporal, material act that leaves behind evidence of its having occurred. Arche-writing describes, according to Sharon Crowley, "human in-scription on the world's surface" (4). As such, it can easily apply to any and all semiotic activity. Furthermore, any and all human activity can be described as semiotic, so one is always arche-writing.

But composition studies knows—or should know—that the details of the relation between arche-writing and narrow writing can be explored, both abstractly and empirically. Doing so might involve intentionally blurring the differences between the two, especially as their relations are pursued empirically, and as one tries to assign empirical dimensions to Derrida's theory of writing. Derrida claims that grammatology cannot be a "positive science," that it has no proper object of study precisely because the subject-object conceptual system is in question (*Grammatology* 74). But precisely because of grammatology, composition theory can recognize and elaborate the writtenness of the empiricist impulse in order to rearticulate empiricism itself as a form of writing. This in turn allows the notion of an "object of study" to become tactical rather than epistemo-ontological.

By redefining concepts as discursive tactics within a general framework of writing, composition theory can move closer toward explaining what writing is and how writing works in the world. Writing happens, and composition researchers can watch it happen and make claims about it, or they can look at the artifacts it leaves behind and make claims about writing as a result. To do so with the disposition for which this book argues is to map the ways in which, for example, an act of writing can be considered a contingent and impossible attempt to fix meaning. It is to show how acts of writing try to present presence, the supposed existence of which is known only through prior acts of writing. This is perhaps most clearly the case in the writing of academic disciplines, which, according to Jonathan Culler, "must suppose the possibility of solving a problem, finding the truth, and thus writing the last words on a topic" (90). But it is equally the case in the economy of such forms of writing as e-mail, or any other genre in which the idea of "the last word" lingers, explicitly or implicitly.

But in most current composition theory, writing is not theorized in this way. In fact, writing is undertheorized when discussed at all. In its place are offered alternative terms such as *discourse, language,* or *signification,* which are variously thought to have more explanatory power than writing. Discourse, in particular, with its Foucauldian resonance, is intended to cover a broader range of culturally embedded signifying functions. Its scope is thought to exceed that of writing.

The motive for such substitutions is understandable. Many composition theorists have sought to connect our field's interests to the cultural practices that comprise an increasingly complex, interconnected, and written world. They have rightly found fault with theories that attend to writing as though it were a discrete activity. And so in an effort to broaden the range, applicability, and potential influence of composition studies, they have changed the object of study on the assumption that the category of *writing* alone cannot describe the theoretical and cultural situations they see before them.

But writing can and does do this work. Furthermore, a reinvestment in writing might contribute to a revival of humanistic inquiry, and therefore of descriptions of human activity, all accounting for writtenness. *Writing* is almost exclusively our field's term, in ways that *discourse, language,* and *signification* are not. Turning the field's intellectual and disciplinary gaze back to writing gives composition studies the ability to articulate writing in new ways. It certainly gives composition studies the chance to move beyond the pervasive paradigm of representation with which the rest of English studies has been so long taken. It permits us to describe writing in different terms than it has heretofore been described.

In asserting that composition studies needs a different disposition toward writing, I recognize, as I noted above, that *theory* is itself a difficult term. I acknowledge that if what I am saying about writing is the case, then there probably is no theory as such, and that rather than theory there is instead writing that comes to be called theory. But the implications of such a predicament are themselves worth exploring, because most of us in composition studies continue to approach theory unproblematically from these outworn Cartesian perspectives that underwrite the representational paradigm. The old rugged *cogito*—the subject with a "mind" capable of perceiving objects "more rigorously and more distinctly"—is so deeply entrenched in composition studies that it is only with difficulty that we recognize it as a subject position at all. We are like the "modern philosopher," whom Dalia Judowitz describes as trying to approach Cartesian reality from a position outside of its long shadow but "whose worldview is so deeply imbued with the notion of subjectivity that it becomes impossible to envisage and describe its origins" (1). We firmly believe, despite our postmodern claims, in the presence of *something else* beyond the veil of language, and we have described it as being fundamentally apart from our language use, and we believe it to be theory's task to define and explain this noumenal realm. Consequently, our inquiries into writing are devoted to articulating the deep divide between the *cogito* and the world. And despite revivals of alternative voices from rhetorical history, such as the Sophists and Giambattista Vico, as well as the decade-long espousal of postmodernism by prominent composition theorists, the field has done little to produce a theory of the writing act that does not carry the epistemic baggage of this Cartesian ideology, filtered most recently through the hermeneutic disposition.

The same problem obtains for our descriptions of the subject, which demands as much theorization as did the traditional reading subject of literary studies. In composition studies, this demand is met, as I will explain in chapter 4, beginning with Janet Emig's *The Composing Processes of Twelfth Graders*, on to Mina Shaughnessy's *Errors and Expectations*, through David Bartholomae's "Inventing the University," and finally to Susan Miller's *Rescuing the Subject*. But, so far, not beyond. These works remind composition studies of its unique project at the same time that they serve as emblems of its difference from the rest of English studies, a difference evident in debates over the field's proper modes of theorizing, which have ranged from an empiricism informed by the natural and social sciences to a rationalism informed by the humanistic disciplines of literary theory and modern philosophy.

Composition's Theory

In light of the difficult theoretical situation I am describing in composition studies, it is disheartening to think of how long composition studies has been engaged with discourses of theory, considering the minimal effect this engagement has had. In fact, the familiar interpretation of composition's theoretical turn, as well as of its earlier empirical orientation, argues that theoretical and methodological diversity is one of the field's strengths. For example, Janice Lauer identifies composition's "multimodality" as a risky but ultimately beneficial characteristic, noting that the field "has maintained from the beginning what a number of disciplines are just starting to admit—that many of their most important problems can be properly investigated only with multiple research methods" (25–26). But it is not clear whether this phenomenon, which Berkenkotter calls "epistemological ecumenicalism," represents a novel attitude toward academic inquiry or a merely haphazard mingling of established theories and procedures (79). In particular, composition theory has exhibited a lack of rigor. As Lynn Worsham notes, many expressions of composition theory recklessly adopt postmodern terminology—including the term *postmodern*—without adequate reflection or contextualization ("Critical" 8). The field has been working at theory for too long to have gotten so little out of it.

For example, while landmark theoretical essays such as Maxine Hairston's "The Winds of Change" and James Berlin's "Rhetoric and Ideology in the Writing Class" can be said to have taught the field to apply existing theories, they did not suggest how to write new ones. This absence is ironic, considering these essays' influence on composition theory. Hairston's may in fact have significantly helped cause the proliferation of composition theory that I am considering here. As we know, Hairston called for more empirical studies to be carried out for the purpose of solidifying what she saw as the field's emerging sense of itself as a discipline. But while empirical studies might have been produced in response to her call, what is arguably most striking, memorable, and influential about that essay is its argumentative strategy. It borrows a theoretical concept from Thomas Kuhn and uses it to describe composition's institutional disposition. Specifically, it puts forth the theoretical notion of the "paradigm shift." In doing so, it inaugurates an enduring method for "doing" composition theory: take a term or concept from a more respected and respectable field such as philosophy and use it to illuminate some aspect of composition studies. Of course, this move was not novel; in the 1970s, people in composition studies had done the same with theory from the social sciences. And even the idea of borrowing from philosophy was not new. But Hairston did not test or otherwise interrogate her theoretical framework before determining its applicability to composition's situation. She stated her understanding of Kuhn's concept and then simply asserted its relevance to the current state of the field. Soon there would be similar essays making similar moves but using different theorists from outside composition studies: Derrida, Foucault, Cixous, Wittgenstein, Irigaray, and so on.[3] The writer would summarize a concept and then assert that the concept shed light on a particular issue relevant to composition. Sometimes the application applied to a theoretical problem, sometimes a pedagogical or even administrative one.

James Berlin's equally influential article, "Rhetoric and Ideology in the Writing Class," enacts a similar strategy, one that contributed to or at least exacerbated the split between theory and empirical research. By aligning what he called "cognitivist rhetoric" with capitalist ideology and the maintenance of an oppressive societal status quo, Berlin promoted a vision of composition that saw philosophical/ideological orientations as being embodied in particular research methods. The practitioners and researchers of cognitivist rhetoric, according to Berlin, were inevitably capitulating to the status quo by virtue of the kinds of questions they asked and the ways they set out to answer them. Berlin's strategy was straightforward: offer a short primer on Louis Althusser's theory of ideology and read current research in composition studies according to that framework. Thus, the essay was not, in itself, a new theoretical work on writing or discourse. Rather, it was an assertion of a relation between critical theory and composition practice. These forms of composition theory, of which Hairston's and Berlin's were only the most visible and persuasive examples, remain the predominant "methods" of theorizing in our field today.

Recently, Flower and others have reasserted the importance of empirically oriented theorizing.[4] Flower's "[o]bservation-based theory building" follows the lead of such feminist philosophers of science as Donna Haraway and Sondra Harding in their call to develop "more adequate images of objectivity" (106). According to Flower, objectivity is not what we thought it to be: an unimpeded view onto a given object. Instead, she argues, it is one of many "vital but limited tools in the rhetorical process of case building" (167). There is much room for disagreement with the particulars of Flower's argument, especially her insistence on a meaningful a priori distinction between cognition and context. But her theoretical point—and more importantly, the methodological implication that follows from it—is worth noting. Once observation (the empirical activity) is understood to be a tool for building arguments rather than as justification of preexisting orientations— once it is articulated as a form of writing—then it becomes not simply necessary but perhaps indispensable to inquiry. Empiricism thus loses its ontological baggage and becomes rhetorical, as Flower underscores the importance of making theoretical arguments rather than assertions. The case she makes for observation-based theory building is an implicit case for treating theory as a form of writing, one in which concepts are proposed, examined—"interrogated"— rather than simply applied. Thus, the possibility arises that composition theory might generate new theories rather than retrofit existing ones. In the following chapters, I hope to achieve a similar goal by emphasizing a theorized version of writing as the key term or *concept* through which most of composition theory's erstwhile concerns are best addressed.

❖2❖

The Discourse of Knowledge in Composition Theory

Composition studies has long claimed that writing repre-sents, emerges from, or helps shape humans' mental, emo-tional, or sociocultural states of being. It has also situated the act of writing at the beginning, middle, or end of the many features that comprise these states of being, and it has investigated writing's particular relation to these features. In sum, composition studies has investigated in detail the proposition that to write is to somehow engage or connect with other aspects, both noumenal and phenomenal, of the world. According to the field's body of knowledge, writing variously represents or helps create *some-thing else*, something that is not itself writing. In particular, a history of composition theory would be a story about reforms, refinements, and occasional revolutions concerning the precise nature of this *something else*, but in no case would it be absent.

Elizabeth Ervin points out that for many in the field, *some-thing else* has been and continues to be *knowledge*. In her entry on the term *epistemology* in Heilker and Vandenberg's *Keywords in Composition Studies*, Ervin claims that "most compositionists accept as commonplace [Ann] Berthoff's assertion that 'Compos-ing is knowing'" (76). And she notes the continuing importance to composition studies of a concept of writing tied to knowledge production, claiming that "discussions of epistemology—pragmatic

and otherwise—are central to our scholarship" (76). The centrality of epistemological concerns—of the discourse of knowledge—
in composition theory is the focus of this chapter. It will argue
that the field's investment in such a discourse has yielded poor
theoretical returns because it has reproduced the Platonically
inspired idea that writing is a notation system, a representation
technology for conveying nondiscursive content. Through a critical engagement with Derrida's theory of writing, it will suggest
for composition theory an orientation toward the study of writing
that contextualizes the discourse of knowledge, thus identifying
knowledge as one of several tactically deployed honorifics be-
stowed upon certain collections of statements and activities.

But in making this argument, I will also be calling into
question the larger assumption that writing is best considered and
studied as an act that points to or participates in *something else*.
This chapter will argue that composition theory should begin
giving up this idea in order to at once broaden and sharpen its
focus on writing as a paradigmatically human activity, one that
encompasses representation but is not limited to it.

As Ervin makes clear, in composition theory it is nearly an
axiom that writing is somehow closely related to knowing, more
so even than with other articulations of the *something else* to
which writing is yoked. The idea that "composing is knowing"
is so central an assumption of our field that one might have
difficulty examining it without risking a reader's bewilderment.
But such an examination is needed if the field is to develop a
theoretical disposition toward writing freed from the philosophical discourse to which it has been tethered at least since the
revival of interest in the *Phaedrus*. In that discourse, writing is
an adjunct practice attending to a bigger achievement, such as
knowledge. But if we would set aside or at least defer this
imperative, we might develop very different theories about writing than we have to date. What follows will trace the epistemic
imperative in a range of scholarly texts from our field, including
those that purport to break with Plato by adopting a postmodern
stance. I hope to make the case that writing can be thoroughly

theorized without recourse to a discourse of knowledge and the ideology of representation, that in fact these are reality strategies thwarting our attempts to theorize writing.

Beyond Epistemology

My call to leave behind the epistemic imperative echoes Richard Rorty's old argument against modern philosophy, wherein he traces the formation of philosophy into a professional discipline whose main concern is to develop a theory of knowledge. In *Philosophy and the Mirror of Nature*, he notes that modern philosophy—defined as a series of arguments *about* and advances *toward* this theory of knowledge—is a relatively recent development, one that emerges in the wake of Kant's work, which clearly differentiates between science and philosophy. According to Rorty, Kant and his followers help establish philosophy as the foundational discipline, the one that can provide intellectual warrants for all other disciplines. One key move in this direction is to articulate epistemology as "a *nonempirical* project," an act of "armchair reflection" (137). Kant does this by positing a priori knowledge, knowledge independent of experience and applicable across disciplines. According to Rorty, Kant "enabled philosophy professors to see themselves as presiding over a tribunal of pure reason, able to determine whether other disciplines were staying within the legal limits set by the 'structure' of their subject matters" (139). In this incarnation, philosophy dealt with the origins and sources of knowledge, now understood as being free of contexts and disciplines, where before these had been the culmination or the ultimate expression of particular investigations. *Knowledge* was now an activity that could be conceived of in the abstract, independent of empirical observation. What remained was to arrive at an explanation of how knowing happened.[1]

From a rhetorical standpoint—specifically, one not wholly indebted to philosophical discourse—such a quasi-metaphysical theory of knowledge is untenable and perhaps even illegible. It reiterates a dualism between essence and appearance by insisting on the presence of a noumenal realm where such things as knowledge reside. Nonphilosophical rhetoric of the kind proposed most recently by Victor Vitanza, Michelle Ballif, and D. Diane Davis cannot read this dualism as such. Instead, it understands language or discursive activity to be the constant and necessary component of human activity. Linguistic activity is the ground from which the very idea of dualism (and of "the noumenal") emerges, and this fact is more important than are any details concerning one aspect or another of dualism itself.

I wish to make a similar claim about writing, which is why I consider the persistence of the epistemic perspective in composition theory to be such a problem. I believe we can best continue our tradition of inquiry into writing by looking at the ways in which writing is a paradigmatically human activity. It is an activity that takes place in and over time, but that has not been theorized in this way due to the persistent influence of philosophical discourse, which deals in the noumenal or the metaphysical—that is to say, with "concepts." In this particular case, *knowledge* is a title, a name, given to valued collections of statements, always and only after the (f)act of their production.

If Rorty is right about the history of epistemology—if epistemology represents philosophy's gambit for breaking free from contextualization—then *knowledge* is more of a historical, political, and rhetorical gesture on the part of philosophy than it is a state of being or a thing in the world. Moreover, if epistemology is a strategy, a discourse, a way of writing—that is, if there's no epistemology as such, only tactical deployments of the epistemic honorific—then we have the option of dealing with it as if it were precisely that, and we can revalue it appropriately. After all, the high value we place on the discourse of knowledge is determined mainly by our willingness not to recognize it as a discourse, our investment in the possibility of there being things "*as such*," and the idea that there are things-in-themselves for us to perceive, following Descartes, "clearly and distinctly." But the term "as such" is itself a tactic, the product of epistemic ideology, the result of a discourse of knowledge. And this discourse of knowledge asserts a strong influence on composition theory that we in the field are not in the habit of recognizing, and one that we do not avoid simply by asserting that *knowledge as such* is located differently—that is, in cognitive or subjective or social realms—or simply by claiming that *knowing as such* is a cultural rather than cognitive phenomenon. This is because the discourse of knowledge itself provides terms for describing a world in which the relationship between terms and the world is basically unproblematic, in which words signify things directly. As tactically deployed epistemic terms presented as concepts, *knowledge* and *knowing* are parts of a strategy *precisely* in which terms can stand for concepts. According to this strategy, the function of terms such as *knowledge* and *knowing* is to mark an idea of the very limit of signification, of the end of mediation and the beginning of "things in themselves," or the inauguration of *something else*. Consequently, in their manifestations, they absorb and reflect the various notions of "something else" held by the composition theorists who invoke them, but they do not necessarily articulate a theory of writing outside the old Platonic framework.

Epistemic Rhetoric

As Berlin and others have noted, Robert L. Scott's 1967 essay, "On Viewing Rhetoric as Epistemic," launched an extended debate in communication studies that continues to this day, one in which many noted rhetoricians have participated.[2] The purpose of the rhetoric-as-epistemic thesis is to counter philosophy's claim of being the "tribunal of pure reason." Its own main claim is that rhetorical activity—discussion, deliberation, argumentation, conversation—produces knowledge just as philosophical investigation arrives at or discovers it. In fact, some versions of the rhetoric-as-epistemic thesis consider philosophical investigation—as well as other kinds of investigation—to be a species of rhetorical activity.

Thus, the very nature of knowledge is contested by epistemic rhetoric. It sees knowledge as a thing made not found, and it asserts that this difference is consequential.

But over the years, some theorists, including Scott himself, have seriously questioned and even tried to abandon if not the spirit then at least the letter of the rhetoric-as-epistemic thesis. While in 1967 Scott claimed that through rhetoric one arrives at knowledge and truth, in 1993 he wishes instead to save rhetoric from "the deadening pall of Truth," and for him this requires abandoning the rhetoric-as-epistemic thesis (133). Toward this end, he is content to dispense with the term *epistemic rhetoric*, in its place offering the familiar term *rhetoric of inquiry*. This alternative term has its own history, one which seems to emphasize the processes of knowledge production rather than knowledge as such, but in doing so it nonetheless takes part in the discourse of knowledge. That is, it reserves conceptual space for knowledge or something like it ("something else") in its theory of rhetoric insofar as *inquiry* itself remains a vaguely defined yet honorific term. In both *epistemic rhetoric* and *the rhetoric of inquiry*, knowledge or something like it is the desired outcome. In trading one term for another, Scott seems to recognize the nagging foundationalism that both underwrites and undermines the rhetoric-as-epistemic thesis. But his terminological exchange does not get rid of it. Rhetoric is still compelled to theorize in light of *something else*, even when the focus shifts to processes rather than products.

In composition theory, the popularity of one or another form of epistemic rhetoric is the most notable and recent example of our field's investment in the discourse of knowledge. By relating writing to knowing and knowledge making, advocates of epistemic rhetoric take up a tradition articulated in the 1970s by Janet Emig and Ann Berthoff who, in very different ways, argued that to write was to do something more than represent preexisting thought.[3] The most recent and influential version of epistemic rhetoric has been Berlin's theory of a *social-epistemic rhetoric*. According to Berlin, the distinguishing feature of social-epistemic rhetoric is its "placement of language, of signifying practices, at the center of the rhetorical act" (138). Furthermore, these practices are said to "precede and circumscribe the entire rhetorical context so that the sender, the receiver, and the message are always already linguistically constructed" (138). Berlin's theory thus echoes those stronger versions of epistemic rhetoric that see rhetoric at or near the center of the human enterprise, intimately involved in basic human activities such as knowledge making.

But neither the centralization of language nor the reconfiguration of "the rhetorical context" in terms of signification is a necessarily "epistemic" gesture, so it is not clear what Berlin means to gain by asserting that his social-semiotic theory of rhetoric is also epistemic. He does not assert that signifying practices are the means of knowledge production, only that they constitute human interaction. The answer to this question might be found in the discussion of epistemic rhetoric in communication studies, where proponents of the rhetoric-as-epistemic theses do see *rhetorical* practices as the means of knowledge production. But that is beyond the scope of this project.

Other Critiques of Epistemic Rhetoric

Of course, I am not the first to question the role of social-epistemic rhetoric in composition studies. Others questioned it more than a decade ago, though for the most part they did not attend to the basic theoretical question of the relation between writing and knowledge. For example, in 1991 Joseph Petraglia suggested that composition theorists had not presented social constructionism and the resulting epistemic rhetoric in their full complexity. Specifically, he took issue with those who espoused epistemic views of rhetoric warranted by social constructionism, claiming that while these theorists offered epistemic rhetoric as a way to think differently about issues in composition, they ignored or were not aware of the various "criticisms and controversies" attending to social theories of knowledge in other disciplines such as communication, philosophy, sociology, and anthropology (96). Taking up the perspectives of those disciplines, Petraglia offered a critique of "the basic premises that seem to underlie composition's conception of social construction" (96). His goal was not to discredit social construction nor to offer the field an alternative to epistemic rhetoric. Instead, it was to point out that so uncritical a reception of so important a claim threatened the field's ability to generate "fresh ideas and critiques" related to that claim (112). As he saw it, this disciplinary "insularity" emerged from the compositionists' otherwise laudable pursuit of a "social justice and empowerment" agenda, one that sought to place at the field's forefront a "concern for the social constraints imposed on the writer" (111). But, Petraglia noted, the criticisms of social theories of knowledge had been "fairly common currency in rhetoric for some time," and for the field to not have taken them into account, to not have allowed them to challenge established theorizations, was to have allowed social construction and epistemic rhetoric to become empty categories (111).

Likewise, that same year, Daniel Royer traced epistemic rhetoric (and composition's interest in it) to long-standing philosophical debates on the nature and development of knowledge, though he stopped short of questioning the nature of knowledge as such and its relation to rhetoric. Instead, he pointed out that these debates were comprised of the realist position that knowledge is the impersonal result of humans' direct observation of the world and the idealist position that knowledge is the personal result of humans' active engagement with the world as presented to them by their sense perceptions. Royer saw epistemic rhetoric, as represented in works such as Knoblauch and Brannon's *Rhetorical Traditions and the Teaching of Writing*, as emerging from the idealist position. He also argued that epistemic rhetoric was thus problematic insofar as the idealist position was fraught with theoretical problems and still widely contested within philosophical circles. According to Royer, epistemic rhetoric also suffered from its advocates' "dogmatic insistence on epistemological superiority," a dogmatism matching that of the realist view of rhetoric it would displace (292). As he saw it, there remained open questions as to "how and when it is that communication creates knowledge and the status of that knowledge," questions that neither a rigid realism nor a rigid idealism and its attendant epistemic rhetoric could resolve (295).

Also in 1991, Victor Vitanza, following Stanley Fish, noted that proponents of social-epistemicism in composition studies, through their "theory hope," had simply reinvented foundationalism along socially oriented lines. Vitanza asserted that these theorists, in addition to being "dangerously utopian and blindly ideological," had "not been suspicious enough of their rationalistic motives, which [were] best described as the will to knowledge and power" (143). He saw in their project an attempt to formulate a Habermasian "critical rationalism" that would arrive at a "legitimation of knowl-edge" through universally understandable and applicable discourse practices (144). Following Lyotard, Vitanza identified this as "the game of knowledge," driven by a "nostalgia for universals" and a belief in "ideal speech acts" (145). In contrast, and again following Lyotard, Vitanza offered countertheses against this newly emerging epistemicism. These would be examples of "a different set of language games," one not tethered to the Enlightenment ideology of totality as embodied in such concepts as *knowledge* and the pseudo-problem of its legitimation in a politically, philosophically, and otherwise fragmented world.

In the years since Petraglia's, Royer's, and Vitanza's essays were published, debate on the social dimensions of knowledge has continued outside composition studies, particularly among rhetoricians in communication studies. But inside composition studies, their warnings seem to have gone unheeded. Granted, few compositionists actively assert or argue for social construc-tion or epistemic rhetoric these days, but this is because they do not need to. The rhetoric-as-epistemic thesis has become part of composition studies' normal discourse, affecting its approaches to its objects of study. Certainly, the field has historical reasons for doing so, as Ervin's essay makes clear. Scholars such as Ann

Berthoff and Peter Elbow had synthesized writing and knowing long before anyone brought epistemic rhetoric to composition studies. So the claim that writing partakes of or participates in "something else," something more humanly essential and intellectually appealing than the practice of writing itself, does not originate with composition's social-epistemic rhetoricians. But they did give the claim theoretical heft at a time in the field's intellectual history—the 1980s and early 1990s—when theory had itself become a valued commodity in the rest of English studies.

As I have noted, following Berlin, the explicit concern over epistemic rhetoric begins in communication studies, specifically with Robert Scott's 1967 article, "On Viewing Rhetoric as Epistemic." At the time that Berlin and others introduced the notion of epistemic rhetoric to composition studies, it was a useful and even necessary foundation on which to build composition theory, a key component of the field's quest for disciplinary and intellectual identity. If writing could be connected to long-standing rhetorical and philosophical issues, then the field would gain legitimacy, much as it had when its researchers in the 1970s had adopted social-scientific methods of empirical inquiry into the writing process. More importantly, such a theory would be a genuine contribution to the growing body of information about writing. But today, despite its continuing presence in composition theory, the status of epistemic rhetoric in communication studies is in doubt, as I have previously noted. And composition theorists need to know why this is the case so that we might begin to consider how well epistemic rhetoric serves our purposes.

In what follows, I will examine some recent works in composition theory, identifying the ways in which the discourse of knowledge informs how the field understands both its object of study and its own research on that object. I will address more recent theoretical works in the field, works that do not argue, as does Berlin, for a specifically epistemic view of writing or rhetoric, but which use the epistemic perspective as a point of departure from which to pursue other objectives.

The Discourse of Knowledge in Composition's Metadiscourse

As its title indicates, Sidney Dobrin's *Constructing Knowledges* operates from an ostensibly nonfoundational approach to the field's conception of knowledge in order to refigure the role of theoretical work on writing. Because of this, the book's object of study is not writing but the means and politics by which research on writing is produced and valued. An analysis of this metadiscourse thus can reveal not how composition theorists study writing but what we think we are doing when we study it. To borrow a phrase from Althusser, it reveals part of our imaginary relationship to our object of study, and as such it is important insofar as it suggests how in turn we actually approach that object: the questions we ask of it, the things we assert that it does. In its discussion of "theory wars" in composition studies, *Constructing Knowledges* offers a glimpse of our sense of what we do, and it reveals that *knowledge* is a debated and debatable topic among us when we reflect on the state and future of our discipline. If *knowledge* occupies as large a space in our collective imaginary as this book suggests, then it may not be surprising to see this concern spilling over into our deliberations about the nature and function of our traditional object of study: writing. It seems, in fact, that composition studies is saturated with the discourse of knowledge. And if this is the case, then articulating an alternative to it might be an impossible task. Still, for reasons I have stated above, it should be pursued.

Constructing Knowledges does not see theoretical work as contributing directly toward a stable body of knowledge, toward a corpus of facts and insights upon which to base, among other things, classroom practice. Instead, it prefers a model of theoretical work that continuously and perpetually fuels further discussion about, among other things, the relation between theory and practice. Entailed in the distinction *Constructing Knowledges* draws between theoretical work as part of an accumulative enterprise and theoretical work as a speculation-generating activity is a related distinction between knowledge as the thing accumulated and knowledge as the necessarily untidy and ever-shifting compilation of positions, assertions, and practices generated by constant speculation and meta-speculation. One shorthand way of describing this difference, as indicated in the book's title, is to say that the former process works toward *knowledge* while the latter deals in *knowledges*. This pluralizing of the term asserts antifoundationalism insofar as it proposes epistemological multiplicity whereby the supposed results of inquiry may assume a range of forms and expressions. According to this approach, to designate something as *knowledge* is to perform an epistemologically contingent, culturo-historico-political act that cannot be adjudicated through recourse to an impartial, disinterested, or objective standard. And so the same spirit of pluralism that understands the processes of theoretical work to be varied also understands the products of theoretical work to be varied. Thus, there are *knowledges*.

It is possible to take issue with the assumptions from which *Constructing Knowledges* proceeds. That is, one could argue against the very idea of *knowledges* as a viable theoretical or even empirical concept by taking up the cause of foundationalism and its preference for theory building toward ever-increasing stores of *knowledge*. But more interesting is how the supposed differences between these two perspectives are eclipsed by their shared dependence on the discourse of knowledge, by their mutual investment in a notion of "something else" that, however conceived or articulated, underwrites their claims to truth (or truths).

The antifoundationalism of *Constructing Knowledges* hinges on a clear distinction between theory building and theorizing, between *knowledge* and *knowledges*. These distinctions are supposed to be consequential precisely to the extent that they signal a radical epistemological shift in composition studies and its disposition toward its objects of study: writing and writing subjects. Yet Dobrin's project is problematic not because it asserts an incorrect epistemology, nor because its antifoundational epistemology turns out to be foundational, but because it asserts epistemology at all. Even though *Constructing Knowledges* stands against the idea of "theory building," it nonetheless stands upon an established and familiar theory of knowledge from which to make its case. If we assume that *knowledge* is a concept rather than a technical term from a historically specific discourse, then it makes sense for composition theorists to see what kind of intellectual and disciplinary purchase they can get on it. This would include modifying it to suit various other intellectual exigencies. Such is the case with *knowledges*, where the epistemic imperative of Cartesian discourse is retained despite a more recent impulse to locate it beyond the borders of the *cogito*. But it is not a concept, strictly speaking. As Foucault has shown, concepts always turn out to be groups of produced statements bound to specific historical exigencies.[4]

Post-Process Theory

In "Paralogic Rhetoric: An Overview," Thomas Kent asserts "an anti-foundationalist and neo-pragmatic view of knowledge formation" on the way to theorizing writing as a form of "communicative interaction" (144). He complains that "many contemporary accounts of writing" present it "as a thing-in-itself, most often a process of one kind or another that can be reduced to a system and then taught" (144). Instead, Kent claims, "the primary motive for the act of writing consists in communication, given of course that what we desire to communicate through writing may entail a wide range of intentions" (144). Furthermore, Kent distinguishes between writing and composition, asserting that while the former "is a kind of communicative interaction," the latter "aims primarily to disclose the elements that constitute the composing process" (149).

Kent's argument illustrates the foundationalism of antifoundationalism, and because of this it also points to larger theoretical problems caused by using antifoundationalism as a frame of reference or even a general principle for theorizing writing. Kent asserts that knowledge is formed rather than discovered or arrived at, thus seeming to distance his position from that of foundationalist thinking. He proposes interpretation as the paradigmatic human activity, thus underscoring the contested or negotiated character of knowledge. And he resists the codifying processes by which knowledge is wrought through communicative interaction, thus emphasizing contingency as a basic state of affairs among humans.

Yet despite its emphasis on the processes of knowledge production, Kent's argument deals also in products, so that at the end of any process of knowledge formation, there will be a knowledge product. That it emerges as the result of discursive interaction rather than strictly rational reflection or empirical investigation is significant, but only to a point. As in Scott's "rhetoric of inquiry," the focus here shifts away from product, but the endgame is still knowledge, and this *knowledge* is no less noumenal or metaphysical for having been made rather than discovered. To make claims about the source of knowledge is to seem to address knowledge as such, but it is instead to reconfirm its status as an honorific term, to reinforce the idea that *knowledge* is a good and desired "thing." In other words, to make such claims about the origins of knowledge is to change its description, but not its valuation nor its status as an essence.

In Kent's essay, the immediate theoretical result of such crypto-foundationalism is a Platonic theory of writing. This is rendered most succinctly in the distinction between writing and composition, as well as in the unequal value attached to each. Writing is an open-ended process of transmitting "what we desire to communicate," while composition consists of "issues such as semantics, style, cohesion, genre, and so forth" (144, 149). In other words, writing is the substance of communication and composition is the means by which such substance is rendered. Both, writing and composition serve "something else."

Post-Pedagogical Theory

In *Breaking Up [at] Totality*, D. Diane Davis presents what she calls "A Rhetoric of Laughter for Composition Pedagogy" (209).

This pedagogy is also a theory of writing—or rather, it is informed by a certain theory of writing—that means to be nonrepresentational. Borrowing from later Derrida and Avital Ronell, Davis argues that "[w]hen writing operates representationally, that is, when writing can be viewed as a making-manifest of reality, it is believed to produce 'safe text,' to operate on the side of 'truth'" (233). On the other hand, she notes, "When representation is suspended, reality is at risk" (233). This risk is precisely what Davis wants to encourage through writing that threatens, rather than accepts, the cultural, institutional, and pedagogical imperative to silence the Other of *meaning*. Her text is worth quoting at length here:

> Writing is most threatening . . . when it interrupts the meaning-making machine and, in the instant of that interruption, opens the possibility for an/Other hearing, a hearing of that which has been drowned out by the workings of the machine itself. It is in the moment of this hearing of the previously UNheard, in the activation of an interruption that exposes the rustlings of finitude, that community—our being-in-common—presents itself. Finitude is exposed in the instant that the myth of common-being is interrupted by the excess it attempts to silence. (234)

For Davis, writing at its most powerful neither presents nor represents ideas, thoughts, or meanings. In fact, as I have been arguing, writing that does such work has been rendered subservient to]one or another supposedly greater goal. Even in composition studies, the field charged with the care and teaching of writing, writing has been thus enslaved, as it were, most often to the discourse of knowledge. Davis notes that "the job of the typical composition course is to perpetuate that myth . . . for the sake of society . . . Reality . . . Truth. For the sake of *knowledge*" (234).

But a problem arises in Davis's proposal for an alternative theorization of writing, a theorization that, shrewdly, means to break with the ideology of representation but that in doing so resorts to a purely abstract articulation of writing to stand in place of now-deposed *knowledge, representation,* and *truth* as the newly unassailable "god term" from which a new discourse would proceed. Davis asks, "What would happen if writing were dismissed from its representational servitude, if, that is, *we put ourselves in the service of writing* rather than the other way around?" (235). Then, in an echo of nineteenth-century aestheticism, she even offers the possibility of a "writing *for writing's sake*" (235). Both of these gestures culminate in the Nietzschean "pedagogy of laughter" she favors, one comprised of a series of familiar gestures valued by postmodern perspectives: parody, pastiche, irony, self-reflection, rhetorical analysis. Unfortunately, by turning to a philosophical aestheticism, Davis's theory of writing situates itself squarely within a strand of the philosophical tradition it might otherwise disdain. In other words, underwriting Davis's theory is a discourse with a narrative thread running through the work of Nietzsche, Deleuze and Guattari, and Cixous that Davis cites. But because of this, her alternative theory's status *as* an alternative within an established ideological system—made up of "traditions" and "countertraditions"—undercuts its own claims to a thorough recasting of writing. Furthermore, it has no empirical dimension.

These problems are underscored by the activities Davis imagines taking place in the new composition classroom, one based on her alternative theorization. "Students," she writes, "would be invited to disrupt their own positions, to contradict themselves, to expose all that must be hidden and excluded in the precious name of clarity" (243). They "would be required . . . to be constantly on the lookout for what each of their various and incompatible discourses is making of them" (244). As with Berlin's descriptions of ideal composition classroom practices, Davis's vision reinstalls a hermeneutics of suspicion and the modernist writing subject required to enact it.

Certainly, there is a substantial difference between the external threat against which James Berlin's hermeneutical writing subject would have to defend and the internal surprise for which Davis's hermeneutical writing subject would have simply to prepare. And this difference may be enough. Or, rather, it may be all composition studies can reasonably expect so long as its pedagogical mission—and thus its identity—remains intact. As others, including Davis, have noted, our field seems to require a stable writing subject upon which to focus its pedagogical will. Otherwise, its very existence is threatened. But perhaps it is still possible to rearticulate that writing subject—and, in turn, that pedagogical mission—in ways not yet fully accounted for. Derrida's theory of writing helps us pursue that possibility.

Derrida, Writing, and Theories of Agency

As I have noted, rather than associate writing with the discourse of knowledge, composition theorists might instead theorize writing as an activity that produces sentences or statements, some of which come to be identified, after their production, as *knowledge*. Writing so theorized would not be an epistemic phenomenon. It would not necessarily be understood as a means to record, discover, or produce—via cognitive, social, or even sociocognitive operations—anything other than more of itself. Writing so theorized would be neither a conduit nor a generator of intelligible things, abstract concepts, or knowledge as such. It would be much more complex, paradigmatic, and comprehensive than any merely epistemic notion could explain. In turn, the terms *knowledge* and *knowing* could denote not states of being nor metaphysical achievements but variously privileged and changing assortments of honorifics assembled and deployed. Their use as terms would be a shorthand for the sorting of sentences and statements, while writing would become at once the generative matrix from which such shorthands emerge as well as the human practice by which they do so. Under such a terminological reorganization, we might still want to say that writing can produce "something else," perhaps something like *knowledge*. But this would be a tactical, rhetorical decision rather than an implicitly philosophical or metaphysical gesture.

In other words, writing is sufficiently interesting and complex when not tied to a discourse that is inherently and historically antirhetorical. In fact, it is more interesting and complex under the conditions I am describing. To date, composition theory has helped turn on its head the idea that writing is only the recording or reporting of knowledge. It has instead asserted that writing produces knowledge. But it has not questioned the terms of the supposed relationship between writing and knowledge; it has only inverted their order. When composition theorists invoke *knowledge* or *knowing* as an important result of writing, we continue to participate, despite our best intentions, in a historical discourse that can only articulate writing as precisely the handmaiden of knowledge. As a result, this otherwise commendable effort to explain the complexity of writing by linking it to the production of knowledge has reasserted writing's ancillary status. It does not matter whether we believe that knowledge precedes language, or that language precedes knowledge, or even that both somehow coexist. In any of these configurations, we continue to work under a paradigm built around a discursive space for *something else*, for things *as such* that make themselves known through discourse. This guarantees that the product of discourse—the product of the act of writing or speaking, the thing that rhetoric generates—will always promise something other than more discourse. It guarantees the reproduction of the philosophical/ideological insistence that "something else" lurks behind the veil of writing, something that it is the job of thought to perceive and writing to record and secure. In such a system, language—and writing— can only ever be a secondary consideration, no matter how often one asserts its primacy.

The lack of attention composition theorists have paid to Derrida's work, and for so long a time, is surprising. As far back as 1988, Jasper Neel's *Plato, Derrida, and Writing* pointed out

Derrida's relevance to our field while lamenting the fact that "American writing theorists" had paid so little attention to his work (100). Now, after the turn of the new century, Neel's claim about Derrida's importance still holds, as does his observation about Derrida's absence in composition theory.[5] But Derrida's deferral of the epistemic question might be the first step out of the Platonic shadow.

For example, in "Signature Event Context," Derrida argues against a theory of communication as the transmission of meaning or content, a theory in which writing is seen as "a species of general communication" rather than a paradigmatic activity (314). He identifies this approach to communication as being part of "a vast, powerful, and systematic philosophical tradition dominated by the self-evidence of the *idea*," and in which the sign functions "as a representation of the idea, which itself represents the perceived thing" (314). In its place, he offers what he calls a "general displacement" of this system, one wherein

> writing no longer would be a species of communication, and all the concepts to whose generality writing was subordinated (the concept itself as meaning, idea, or grasp of meaning and idea, the concept of communication, of sign, etc.) would appear as noncritical, illformed concepts, or rather as concepts destined to ensure the authority and force of a certain historic discourse. (314–15)

For Derrida, the specific features of writing as we normally understand it—its iterability or "essential drifting" (316), its ability to break with an original context, its separation from a present referent, its citationality—are also the features of all language and of what is called, philosophically, Being. He sees activities such as *knowing*, which philosophical tradition urges us not to imagine as "technical" and therefore secondary but rather as ontological or perhaps epistemological and therefore primary, as being authorized, as it were, by writing. In other words, without the (f)act of writing, the category of *knowing* has no meaning, does no work.

For composition theory, this perspective on writing is in one sense an affirmation of long-held theoretical notions, but it is also a challenge to unquestioned assumptions. And while I am mainly interested in the challenges posed for composition theory, I want first to highlight the important affirmation such a perspective provides.

First, Derrida's theory of writing, while certainly not rooted in theories of cognition, nonetheless helps affirm composition's investment in the idea of writing as a mode of learning insofar as it too rejects traditional representational theories of meaning. The writing-as-learning thesis, as articulated by Janet Emig, sees writing as a complex and integrated activity through which humans combine "enactive," "iconic," and "symbolic" ways of reckoning with the world in order to *make* meaning and personal knowledge (10). As such, this thesis argues that writing is—or should be—a paradigmatic activity, a way of coming to terms with the world—a way of knowing or coming to know a body of knowledge, whether academic or otherwise. It rejects the idea that meaning is something primarily transmitted, an idea that Derrida equally rejects as he establishes the primacy of a noncommunicational writing that "does not give rise to a hermeneutic deciphering, to the decoding of meaning or truth" but that instead generates systems of meaning as effects or categories of its own unending iterability ("Signature" 329).

Second, Derrida's skepticism concerning the idea of *communication* is echoed by Ann Berthoff, who sees the concept as flawed but nonetheless "protected by its presumed scientific status" (53). It is flawed, according to Berthoff, because it allows people in composition to confuse *information* with *meaning*, treating the latter as though it were merely the product of code, thus resulting in uninformative and scientistic research which in turn yields skills-oriented pedagogies that treat writing as a strictly linear and utterly unimaginative process. Likewise, Derrida questions the viability of the very idea of communication insofar as it presupposes that "the content of the semantic message" can be transferred "within a homogenous element across which the unity and integrity of meaning is not affected in an essential way" (311). Finally, Derrida's theory helps raise writing to the valued level of the epistemological, equating writing and knowing in the same way that Berthoff had sought to do in her attempts to theorize the imagination as the faculty that animates both processes. Writing in this instance is not "merely" technical; it is the means by which a valued process, *knowing*, and a valued product, *knowledge*, come about. Writing seen in this way is an agent of the imagination, and for Berthoff, following I. A. Richards, the imagination is "the chief speculative instrument—that is, a powerful idea to think *with* as well as *about*" (28). It is not simply the recorder of preexisting data, facts, or information.

Yet despite these affirmations, Derrida's theory of writing ventures beyond them, prompting us to ask different questions. Specifically, it prompts us to look past the epistemological, and therefore beyond considerations of *knowing* and *knowledge*. Where Berthoff's theory imagines an equal relationship between writing and knowing enacted on the stage of the imagination, Derrida's theory allows us to suppose not only that knowing is an effect or product of writing, but also that the *idea* of knowing is a discursive effect or product of writing. That is, Derrida's theory suggests that *knowing* is one of those concepts "destined to ensure the authority and force of a certain historic discourse," the discourse Rorty called modern philosophy (315). A theory of writing does not need to be bound to this historic discourse. In fact, the extent to which it is bound to such a discourse will be the extent to which it is unable to say something about writing that will not have been prescribed by the *Phaedrus*.

But for a composition theorist, the prospect of such a theory of writing raises the question of the subject, the question of agency. Both writing-as-notation and writing-as-knowing offer profiles of a writing subject familiar to people in composition studies. In the former, the writing subject is a secretary, sorting and recording the products of epistemological activities that have already occurred.

In the latter, the writing-subject is a quasi-romantic figure for whom the act of writing is an epistemic exploration of individual and/or collective cultural practices. For Derrida, the iterability and citationality that characterize writing—the always already repeated and repeatable nature that marks writing as the paradigmatic human activity—assume an almost foundational quality, and he insists that these features are not to be imagined as options to an otherwise stable system of reference. It is not a question of iterability/citationality and something else, but of different iterations:

> Thus, one must less oppose citation or iteration to the noniteration of an event, than construct a differential typology of forms of iteration, supposing that this is a tenable project that can give rise to an exhaustive program. . . . (326)

The "exhaustive program" suggested here seems to point to some kind of empirical investigation, resulting in a mapping or organizing of the various "forms of iteration" one might find. Such work would clearly be recognizable to people in composition. But such an investigation would not answer the question of agency. Where would one look? What would one look at? Derrida has little to say on the subject, stating only that in such a typology, "the category of intention will not disappear; it will have its place, but from this place it will no longer be able to govern the entire scene and the entire system of utterances" (326). There will be, it seems, a limited notion of agency informing the new theory of writing. But in what way and to what degree it is limited, Derrida does not say.

This is, of course, the same problem that has long plagued postmodern and poststructural theories: the idea that agency or subjectivity cannot be adequately theorized without recourse to some now-deconstructed tenet, principle, or assumption. *The subject* seems difficult to theorize without leaning on assumptions now pejoratively referred to as "modernist," "Enlightenment," or "Platonic." It is a particularly acute problem in composition studies, which proceeds from the premise that "the entire scene and the entire system of utterances" can in fact be governed, or at least recognized, by an agent. Early research into what would be called the writing process was meant to give teachers more information for improving their students' control over their own writing, to allow students to "own" their texts and discourses. Even the student writer imagined in James Berlin's ostensibly postmodern pedagogy exerts control over given rhetorical situations, paradoxically, by recognizing the degree to which she is controlled by them. In past theories of composition, even those theories seeking to portray writing in its fullest possible complexity, the epistemologically coherent and ontologically unified writing subject has stood fast. In this way, as Lester Faigley notes in *Fragments of Rationality*, composition theory is more closely aligned with modernism than postmodernism (14–15).

In "Agency and the Death of the Author," John Trimbur reiterates the modern/postmodern problematic in composition theory and offers what he calls "A Partial Defense of Modernism" to address the question of agency in our field. He asks "whether we really need—or even can have—a new theory of agency to explain literate acts and literate practices," and he asserts that the very wish for such a theory "grows out of the empty feeling left by the death of the author and the deconstruction of the transcendental subject" (285, 287). He proposes that if we "think of representations of agency not as theories but as structures of feeling," then we will see these representations as being "not the result of determining how to formulate and apply a rule (or a theory) but of our feelings about the possibilities of consequential action and how we recognize and justify what we do" (287, 288). As Trimbur suggests, Raymond Williams's theory of "structures of feeling" is rich and complex, and because of this it wields a great deal of analytic power. But Trimbur puts forth this concept as though it were not itself a theory, thus allowing him to advance his claim that a theory of agency is neither needed nor possible. "Structures of feeling" in this argument is a replacement for postmodern theory, and by implication for theory itself. It is a "notion," as he calls it, that helps explain agency without theorizing it out of existence as postmodern theory has supposedly done.

Trimbur's proposal is conceptually incoherent, but more relevant to my argument is its dependence on the discourse of knowledge, a dependence it shares with the postmodern perspective it would critique. Both Trimbur's essay and Thomas Rickert's postmodern-affiliated response to it assert and naturalize a consequential difference between *modernism* and *post modernism*, after which each takes sides. Thus, they participate in a conversation where the idea of agency is important, and it is important precisely because of its relation to the idea of *knowledge*: the modern side dictates an epistemologically autonomous subject, and the postmodern side dictates an epistemologically connected one. Both assume an epistemological framework within which *agency* becomes a central concern. Rickert, for example, worries that Trimbur's argument "sneaks foundationalism back into epistemology," and as an alternative he offers a "posthuman epistemology" that embraces the antagonisms Trimbur's argument tries to avoid (679, 681).

As I have noted, composition studies is perhaps the field most invested in the idea of agency, and this investment influences even the most postmodern of our theoretical expressions. But as long as the field continues to pursue such distinctions, distinctions sanctioned by the discourse of knowledge, it will only be able to address a very limited range of issues and concerns about writing. And at any rate, a "postmodern" writing subject in composition studies was already articulated more than a decade ago in Susan Miller's *Rescuing the Subject.* Miller pointed out that both modern and postmodern theories offered "technical models for a speaker and a writer . . . despite their radically limited concern with the situations that actual writers face" (11). Then she went on to theorize a writer "who is not the author," that is, who is not imagined to be "an independent, potentially totalizing, univocal source of statements" (14, 15). This writer inhabits "a complex textual world" and "both originates with, and results from, a written text" (15). Most importantly, this writer performs; specifically, he or she "performs an assertion by inscribing language" (15). The performance temporarily fixes *meaning*—another terminological artifact of the discourse of knowledge, I might add—but this meaning neither originates in nor proceeds from the writer. To write, according to Miller, is to "stabilize fluidity," the inexorable movement of textuality, on the assumption that communication happens. It is, as Miller notes, to "re-present presence," suspending for a moment the impossibility of presence.

I will pursue Miller's argument in the next chapter, which examines composition theory's investment in the discourse of ideology. After that, chapter 4 will again and in more detail address the question of agency, as I consider how two examples of cultural theory outside of composition studies may help our field take its next important theoretical step. For now, it may be enough to say that composition's modernist theory of agency has been underwritten, at least in part, by the discourse of knowledge. The quest for *something else* to be achieved or discovered through the act of writing has been carried out by the quasi-heroic figure struggling to make or discover meaning by means of this technology.

⊹3⊰

Composition's Ideology Apparatus

James Berlin's theory of ideology has been an influential and explicit attempt to reorient composition's approach to its objects of study: writing and writing subjects. It has underwritten a range of theoretical and empirical research on the cultural and institutional dimensions of writing.[1] But that theory's understanding of both rhetoric and ideology emerges from a representationalist paradigm in which writing is principally a vehicle or instrument. Specifically, Berlin situates a hermeneutic theory of rhetoric within an ontological theory of ideology, understanding the former as a means for the dissemination of and resistance to the latter, which is culturally pervasive. His argument is informed by Louis Althusser's Marxist-structural theory of ideology as articulated in "Ideology and Ideological State Apparatuses," and here too, ideology is theorized as an overarching presence around which all other human activity is organized. This chapter reexamines Berlin's and Althusser's attempts to theorize ideology, and it argues that because their understandings of ideology are nondiscursive, they sanction a theory of writing as the notation system of thought and culture rather than the production of sentences and statements that come to be identified, retrospectively, as thought and culture. They also preclude the theorization of writing subjects as thoroughly textual entities.

This is not to say that I mean to set up the too-familiar opposition between postmodernism and Marxism, one wherein Marxism loses. I am not necessarily interested in ridding composition

41

theory of ideology. On the contrary, I agree with Gayatri Spivak who, in *A Critique of Postcolonial Reason*, writes that a theory of ideology "is necessary for an understanding of constituted interests within systems of representation" (252).[2] Such a theory can help compositionists ask more fruitful questions about the production of culture than we have to date asked, and these questions might help us theorize writing subjects as functions of textual activity rather than as essential precursors to it. So theorized, writing subjects would be understood as organizations of writing. Acts of writing would be considered acts of subject formation (and reformation). It is within this broader framework of writing that more familiar discussions of meaning and representation—questions that theories of ideology address—will make theoretical sense: that is, when we understand acts of writing not as ontological afterthoughts but as the generators of such terms as "ontology" itself.

This framework is a theoretical stance toward the production, reception, and circulation of writing that acknowledges writing's role in the making of what come to be called cultures, as well as the subjects that inhabit these cultures. By reexamining ideology theory and the uses to which it has been put in composition, I hope to complicate our understanding of the relationship between our objects of study—writing and writing subjects—and the already-written contexts into and out of which they emerge. Composition theory should have already begun accounting for the increasingly complex and interweaving streams of writing that comprise Western societies. This accounting may not happen without a theory of ideology, but it certainly will not happen without a fundamentally different disposition toward writing. The fact that this disposition has yet to be fully articulated should not prompt us, however, to install a overreaching theory of ideology in its place as we try to address the many functions of writing.

"Rhetoric and Ideology in the Writing Class"

In "Rhetoric and Ideology in the Writing Class," Berlin defines ideologies as "competing discursive interpretations" of the world, each vying for power against the others (478). Ideology is "inscribed in language practices, entering all features into our experience" (479). "A rhetoric," in turn, always carries with it an ideological perspective, or perhaps several; it is not "a disinterested arbiter of the ideological claims of others" (477). Berlin's attachment of articles to the term *rhetoric* (*a* rhetoric, *the* rhetoric) but not to the term *ideology* makes clear the essay's understanding of their relationship. By positing and detailing a specific rhetoric among many possible rhetorics, it situates rhetorical activity solely in local situations while foregoing a general discussion of rhetoric. Doing so allows Berlin to identify a manifestation of rhetoric and then name as ideological the apparently generalizable features inherent in that specific instance. In other words, a rhetoric functions for Berlin as the specific effect of ideology. This means, for example, that something like "expressionistic rhetoric" can be so named, and it can be said to enact a program that values "the pursuit of self expression in intellectual or aesthetic pursuits" while simultaneously denying the possibility of collective or social action (487).

My point is not necessarily that Berlin is wrong about expressionistic rhetoric. Rather, it is that such a statement becomes possible only when rhetoric is understood as a form that carries a preexisting reality content, identified here as ideology. Berlin's analysis depends upon a traditional, hermeneutic theory of rhetoric as a historically specific application of ideological content. More to the point, it relies on the absence of a comprehensive theory of writing. For Berlin, rhetoric is a feature in and of language, but language is not a constitutive feature of reality. If it were, ideology's scope would perhaps be restricted to that activity that can be articulated by individuals, collectives, and social formations. But Berlin makes large claims for ideology, which forces him to make small claims for rhetoric and, more importantly, to miss an opportunity to establish a theory that might explain the formation of textually embedded writing subjects and acts of writing. Such a theory might avoid the implicit adherence to a reality principle that characterizes ideology theories: the assumption that there are motives outside and independent of language that manifest in and can be apprehended through the medium of language, the insistence on an unbracketed reality that makes ideology theories, according to Jean Baudrillard, "discourses of *truth*" (*Simulacra* 27). Ideology theory in this vein is an attempt to look behind, to get around, to see through what is apparent on the surface of language and to get at the real. It is the kind of rationalistic theory that underwrites what Michelle Ballif calls "the insidious foundationalism" of the social-epistemic position to which Berlin's work adheres, and which harbors three related "presuppositions":

> that (1) there must be something: ideology the social, "material" conditions, the individual, individual rights, freedom, the dialectic (for example), and (2) it must be able to be known (thus rational), and (3) it must be able to be communicated (thus language and subjects are already presupposed to be rational). (156)

But if instead we forego this version of ideology theory and its attendant demands, instead identifying writing as that which explains the production (or location) of topics—of which ideology theory is but one—then ideology becomes not a "something" but a function or effect.

It might be possible to read "Rhetoric and Ideology in the Writing Class" as a prelude to a conversation among theorists in the composition community. Such a reading allows us to see Berlin's work as a text intended mainly to call attention to the relationship between rhetoric and ideology and to offer some initial ideas on that subject. Even were it so, this reading would not exempt the work from scrutiny, an exemption based on the notion that such scrutiny misses the point. Furthermore, its reception in the field has focused on its pedagogical and political implications rather than theoretical questions as such. Responses have tended to apply, extend, or complicate Berlin's ideas about the classroom, or they have pointed to contradictions between Berlin's theoretical apparatus and his political commitments. For example, Marshall Alcorn claims that "Berlin's account of the postmodernist classroom labors to overcome a variety of contradictions that repeatedly subvert the theoretical rigor of his argument" (339). And on the other hand, Michael Murphy points to "the latent and largely disabling residue of progressivist libertarianism in Berlin's work" that counters his otherwise "deliberate, self-conscious, and carefully theorized assault on the cultural orientation of traditional composition pedagogy" (217). But unlike Alcorn, Murphy, and others, I am interested in the "theoretical rigor" of Berlin's argument.[3] So while I appreciate the fact that essays such as "Rhetoric and Ideology in the Writing Class" allowed composition theorists to bring a theory of ideology to their discussions about writing, I also find it troubling that, for the most part, composition theorists have not examined the details of such a combination. Finally, while it is the case that Berlin's last published book, *Rhetorics, Poetics, and Cultures*, moves into new and challenging areas of inquiry—specifically, the assertion of cultural studies as the master trope for a new version of English studies—it is equally the case that its author's previous theoretical and political commitment to the subordination of rhetoric within ideology continues there, and therefore cannot be rationalized as the opening salvo in a discussion of rhetoric and ideology that, at any rate, has not yet taken place.

Rhetorics, Poetics, and Cultures

In *Rhetorics, Poetics, and Cultures*, Berlin asserts once again that "[i]n considering any rhetoric, it is necessary to examine its ideological presuppositions" (77). Thus, the subordination of rhetoric to ideology continues where it had left off in "Rhetoric and Ideology in the Writing Class," as Berlin turns to Göran Therborn's *The Ideology of Power and the Power of Ideology* for an extension of Althusserian ideology theory that includes "structuralist and poststructuralist formulations" (78). According to Berlin, Therborn incorporates the work of Foucault and Gramsci into that of Althusser, which makes Therborn's method "at every turn rhetorical, by which I mean he considers ideology in relation to communicators, audiences, formulations of reality, and the central place of language in all these" (78).

But the difference between Berlin's interpretation of Therborn and Berlin's interpretation of Althusser is not as great as he would have it, particularly on the question of interpellation. In describing Therborn's theory, Berlin notes that ideology "brings with it strong social and cultural reinforcement, so that what we take to exist, to have value, and to be possible seems necessary, normal, and inevitable—in the nature of things" (78). This is a reiteration of the ideology-as-mystification thesis that lingers in the background of Althusser's work due to its own differentiation between science and ideology. I will address Althusser's work in more detail below, but at this point it is necessary to note that Berlin's reading of Therborn makes Therborn look like Althusser, insofar as both contain this residual, pre-Althusserian element. And actually, Berlin is nearly right to confuse the two. I don't want to pursue the details of Therborn's theory in this essay, but it might be enough to say that because Therborn's theory uses Althusser's contributions as a point of departure ("it begins from them," he writes [*Ideology of Power* 7]), it too contains some of the problems I will address below.

Nonetheless, Therborn is explicitly concerned with abandoning the science/ideology distinction, thus differentiating his project from Althusser's (*Ideology of Power* 8–10). And it is also the case that he wants to theorize ideology in conjunction with power, and this is where Berlin identifies an extra dimension that Althusser's theory lacks: access to the discourse of resistance and deployment by already-interpellated subjects. According to Berlin, the "strong cultural and social reinforcement" that attends to ideology also attends to power, as "ideology naturalizes certain authority regimes . . . and renders alternatives all but unthinkable" (78). In this ideology/power matrix, "the subject is a point of intersection and influence of various conflicted discourses," as ideology/power never consolidates its hold on the discursive field (78). Because of this incompleteness, the subject becomes more than a mere function of one discursive regime. According to Berlin, the subject in this scenario becomes "an agent of change" who "negotiates and resists codes rather than simply accommodating them" (78–79). Berlin here is articulating a hermeneutic theory of ideology that posits a relationship of alienation between the subject and society, one in which the former is imbricated in the latter but not necessarily a participant in the making of it. Under such a theory, writing can be theorized only as the notation system of experience—and rhetoric only as the dress of thought—in the subject's ongoing struggle to "negotiate" between acceptable and unacceptable codes. And the criterion of acceptability is one's experience of reality, the codification or symbolization of which is open to misrepresentation, which is precisely what the subject needs to avoid. Seen through such a hermeneutic framework, the signs of culture threaten to overtake the subject and must therefore be "decoded" in order for that subject to determine the ways in which they impinge upon its relation to reality and other subjects. So, through better interpretations that misrepresent less perniciously, the subject can come to understand and perhaps eventually resist the claims being made upon it by the dominant forces of cultural (re)production. In other words, if you know what's really going on, you are in a position fight against it. This teaching of an interpretive disposition modeled on what Paul Ricoeur calls "the school of suspicion" has become a popular pedagogy in composition (32). In fact, one version of it finds expression in Berlin's statement of purposes for the "Codes and Critiques" writing course described in"*Rhetorics, Poetics, and Cultures*:

> The effort is to make students aware of cultural codes, the competing discourses that influence their positioning as subjects of experience. Our larger purpose is to encourage students to negotiate and resist these codes . . . to bring about more democratic and personally humane economic, social, and political arrangements.

> From our perspective, only in this way can students
> become genuinely competent writers and readers. (116)

As this passage makes clear, "discourse" and "experience" are
two different phenomena, for Berlin. The former exerts a con-
trolling "influence" on the latter but does not constitute it. That
is, experience is not a function or effect of discourse, though
it can be manipulated by discourse. This assumption of a space
between discourse and experience (and by implication: language and reality, word and thing) authorizes precisely the
hermeneutics of suspicion that Berlin's pedagogy calls for. To
be a "genuinely competent" writer and reader, in this case, is
to distinguish between discourse and experience, and to know
that there are cultural forces that try to keep you in the dark
about that distinction.

As Charles Paine notes in *The Resistant Writer*, this pedagogy of resistance to dominant culture has historical precedent
in a particular form of rhetoric instruction. He notes that "[f]rom
Isocrates and Plato to Burke to contemporary composition theory,
rhetorical training has sought to endow students with the where-
withal to resist the powerful discourses of a culture that seeks
everywhere to inhabit them" (10). According to Paine, in its
current form this tradition calls upon students to "resist the 'subject positions' imposed upon them" (16). But, he argues, one
irony of this resistance pedagogy is that students might see the
pedagogy itself as the thing being imposed, the invader to be
resisted: "While we may think our students have merely con-
formed to the penetrations of commodity culture, we have to
remember that those cultural beliefs, as far as our students are
concerned, are *their* beliefs, and that our countercultural intru-
sions are the alien ones" (16).

Furthermore, in a recent critique of Berlin's pedagogical
project of decoding and resistance, Susan Miller notes that "[b]y
teaching texts rather than their making, by teaching awareness
rather than rhetoric, and by teaching the power of meanings
rather than the making of statements, we inadvertently reproduce

a politics that is aware but passive" ("Technologies" 499). Miller suggests that composition may have taken this turn toward "cultural hermeneutics" in order "to give its work, and its workers, professional parity" in the field of English (500). If so, then composition may have done little more than ape the rest of English studies because, as she notes, "culture as an object of study—no matter how it is studied—no more motivates active literate practices than does reading great literature" (499). If it mistakes ideological analysis for textual production, composition helps arm students with new ways of reading the world. But reading the world is not the same as writing (in) it.

"Ideology and Ideological State Apparatuses"

As my discussion of Berlin's work suggests, even in the work of that compositionist most closely identified with ideology theory, there is no sustained attempt to engage the idea of ideology critically. It has not been scrutinized, questioned, or evaluated before its application, nor has it been analyzed in terms of composition's own theoretical interests in writing. For example, the theory of the subject necessitated by Althusser's theory of ideology has not been questioned from a perspective specific to composition studies, yet his theory of ideology informs a great deal of theoretical work in the field (through Berlin and others). But Althusser's subject is theorized explicitly, so it is important for composition theorists to understand and interrogate it closely before applying it or one of its many derivatives to our own concerns about how to theorize writing subjects. In what follows, I'll try to begin that interrogation process.

    "Ideology and Ideological State Apparatuses" combines psychoanalytical and Marxist terminology in an attempt to theorize ideology as something more than a merely superstructural phenomenon. This is the theoretical innovation for which Althusser is perhaps best known. Althusser contends that ideology does not represent people's *real* conditions of existence. Rather, ideology represents "the *imaginary* relation of those individuals to the real relations in which they live" (162, emphasis added). Through this use of Jacques Lacan's terminology, Althusser tries to attenuate Marxism's traditional "false consciousness" thesis by softening the hard distinction between base and superstructure. By situating ideology as a state or event within the realms of the symbolic and the imaginary, he can now theorize ideology as a structure that underlies both reality *and* the psyche. Ideology theorized in this way becomes extraordinarily complex and pervasive, and the question of its origins and perpetrators becomes very difficult to address. Althusser's innovation marks a significant theoretical moment in the history of ideology theory, but it is also a problematic political moment because of the theory of the incapacitated human subject that it necessitates. Althusser's theory transgresses the heretofore stable boundary between individual and society, thus radically refiguring the space of agency, of the subject. Consequently, tension emerges between the theoretical and the political in the ISAs essay that is of consequence to composition theory, specifically to a theory of the writing subject. I point this out because it seems to me that composition theories have traditionally contained implicit theories of the subject (which chapter 4 will examine in greater detail). But it is not self-evident that Althusser's structural theory of ideology articulates the kind of subject needed for a theory of writing that ventures away from representationalism. In any event, our field has yet to do the necessary work of finding out.

Now, in *For Marx*, which predates the ISAs essay, Althusser does connect ideology to social agency, thus proposing a subject that composition theory might find useful. Althusser writes:

> So ideology is not an aberration or a contingent excrescence of History: it is a structure essential to the historical life of societies. Further, only the existence and the recognition of its necessity enable us to *act* on ideology and *transform* ideology into an instrument of *deliberate action* on history. (232, emphasis added)

As the words I have emphasized indicate, this theory is closely and immediately placed in relation to action or practice. And in still another essay, "Lenin Before Hegel," Althusser cites Lenin's emphasis on practice as a crucial contribution to Marxist theory, pointing to Lenin's claim that philosophy "is a *practice* of political *intervention* carried out in a theoretical form" ("Lenin before Hegel" 107). These emphases on action and practice indicate that, for Althusser, ideology is a phenomenon about which something can be *done*, despite its pervasiveness. That is, ideology can be enacted or resisted by subjects, even though it is always in play. But what remains unarticulated in Althusser's work is a thorough account of the methods by which resistance is enacted by and through subjects, either as individuals or as collectives. I would argue that to speak of such methods as they relate to language is to speak of writing. In other words, if it is true that ideology can be enacted and/or resisted, and if this occurs as the writing of texts, then the compelling questions for composition theory to ask are: "How does the act of generating discourse—specifically, the act of writing—produce and circulate effects that, always and only in retrospect, come to be termed ideological? And what are the features of a subject that generates this activity?"

Althusser Without Guarantees:
The Birmingham Centre's Theory of Ideology

So, for compositionists, the part of Althusser's theory that sees ideology as practice can be of interest because it becomes, in turn, a way to think about writing. On the other hand, the part of his theory that sees ideology as what amounts to an ontology should be of less interest for two reasons. First, ideology-as-ontology does not stand up to analytical scrutiny, especially when language is taken into account. Second, it is unnecessary. Althusser tries to hold the two visions of ideology in tension, but we can see that the attempt to do so is itself an effect of a hermeneutic imperative to account for some motivating force behind the process of signification. In the 1970s, Stuart Hall and others at the Centre for Contemporary Cultural Studies tried to work through this tension and, following Althusser, distinguished between the singular and plural forms of the word as a way of pursuing the matter further. I do not believe that they resolved the problem, but their elaboration of Althusser's ideology as practice gives composition theorists a way to begin thinking about ideology theory in more useful ways.

In an important but unfortunately out-of-print volume from 1978 titled *On Ideology*, originally published in 1977 as *Working Papers in Cultural Studies #10*, Stuart Hall and other members of the Centre collaboratively address the question of ideology from a variety of perspectives, focusing in part on such figures as Marx, Lukács, Gramsci, Althusser, and others. Their discussion of Althusser highlights "his concern for rationality and scientificity" and his project to rid Marxist theory of its residual but still powerful humanist and historicist tendencies (77). They note that although his definitions and uses of ideology vary, Althusser identifies ideology as a "level" in the social formation, residing along with the political level in the superstructure, while the economic level comprises the base. They point out that the relationship between base and superstructure forms a unity "in which we find that the economic determines, *in the last instance*, the political and ideological levels but at the same time is *overdetermined* by each of them" (79). They also note that Althusser "distinguishes between the element in a social formation which is determinant (which is always the economic) and that which is dominant" (79). This for him is a way of maintaining the fundamental role of the base while acknowledging and accounting for the complexity of relations between base and superstructure. They argue that Althusser's writings comprise "an attack on vulgar, economistic and technologistic tendencies within marxism" that reduce and oversimplify relationships between the levels of the social formation by imposing a "crass determinism of the base on the superstructures" (83). In contrast to formulations of ideology arising from these tendencies and which consign it "to the surface of appearances," Althusser stresses equivalences between levels, arguing that each has power to influence the other, despite the fact that the economic is always determinant (83). This is perhaps an overly optimistic reading of Althusser, who seems to be trying to have it both ways, as it were, by stressing equivalent levels on the one hand and final determinants on the other. Nevertheless, this reading does highlight and elaborate the tension that will eventually lead them to Gramsci and the theory of hegemony.[4] Still, if the authors of *On Ideology* are right, then Althusser's ideology theory is perhaps not so overarchingly structural/ontological after all. Granted, Althusser claims that it is an ahistorical and overdetermining force that is difficult to identify, but in fact it is never impossible to identify because the concept of ideology is articulated in *ideologies*, which themselves are embodied in institutions or apparatuses. Ideologies, then, can be located and resisted. In fact, according to Althusser, such resistance is the task facing theory and philosophy in the service of the class struggle.

But this reading suggests that ideology as such is of a fundamentally different order than are ideologies. It suggests that we are talking about two different things, not two versions of the same thing. Simply put, "ideology" cannot address specific applications arising from specific sets of relations, but there are plenty of "ideologies," and we need only look at both large-scale and everyday struggles between people and institutions to find them. The analytical and critical work of the Birmingham Centre—and of cultural studies in general—gets done on the terrain of "ideologies," which is actually the terrain of hegemony. And ultimately, Gramsci's theory of hegemony, which pre-dates Althusser's ideology by some forty years, is of more use to cultural studies as an analytic for the interpretation of culture. Likewise, hegemony might in the end prove to be a more helpful tool than ideology for the theorization of writing. Unfortunately, with the important exception of Victor Villanueva's discussion of Gramsci in *Bootstraps*, composition's engagement with hegemony theory has yet to occur in any sustained way.[5]

Interpellating the Subject:
Judith Butler on Althusser's Ideology

In his adoption of Therborn's ideology theory, Berlin describes a situation in which subjects are confronted with competing ideologies in which they are imbricated. The fact of dominance and subordination ensures that negotiating will not be easy, will not simply be a matter of individual choice. In fact, the ability to choose will have to be struggled for, and these choices will be understood as also ideologically driven. But the problem of interpellation remains unresolved in Berlin's description of the relationship between subjects and ideologies, and it is a problem that traces back to Althusser: If the subject is a "point of inter-section," a product or function of ideological activity, how can we also say that it is interpellated into ideology without supposing that it has some form of pre-ideological status or existence?

Judith Butler addresses precisely this question, through an analysis of Althusser's ISAs essay, in *The Psychic Life of Power.* Here, she asks the following question of the relation between the hailed/interpellated/constituted subject and the "call" or "voice" to which it responds: "What kind of relation already binds these two such that the subject knows to turn, knows that something is to be gained from the turn? How might we think of this 'turn' as prior to subject-formation, a prior complicity with the law without which no subject emerges?" (107). In other words, she wants to address the nature of this pre-subject from which the subject is said eventually to emerge, after the interpellative act, after the subject is hailed into discourse. Butler's analysis is important for compositionists insofar as it makes vivid, once more, the key problem of Althusser's ideology theory: its imperative to distinguish decisively between discourse and experience, between language and reality, between word and thing.

Butler tries to address this problem by calling attention to the theological terminology that sustains Althusser's theory. She argues that for Althusser, social interpellation takes on the character of a "divine performative" in which "the 'voice' of ideology, the 'voice' of interpellation," like the voice of God, cannot be refused (110). Butler suggests that the voice's act of naming—interpellating—cannot be carried out without "a certain readiness or anticipatory desire on the part of the one addressed" (111). You must be *ready* to receive the Word, if you are to receive It at all. This possibility of a relation prior to interpellation, and of a preexisting desire on the part of the pre-subject, suggests to Butler that the interpellation scene is "belated and redoubled," a reenactment of what has already been determined, and that is now narrativized in discourse, through grammar (111). There is no way, in other words, to render syntactically the emergence of the Althusserian subject without resorting to the grammatical subject. There is no way to express extragrammatically that which is itself extragrammatical.

But Butler's theory of redoubling carries a hint of nostalgia for the idea of a prediscursive subject, and so it might be better simply to say that without the grammatical subject there is no other subject to speak of. True, this grammatical subject, like all signifiers, points to, leaves a trace of, some signified; but this means that the Althusserian theory of subject-formation (i.e., the interpellation of pre-subjects into ideology and discourse) turns out to be an origin story, the story of the first instance (rather than the last), the beginning of signification. And if contemporary theorists are still trying to work through this problem, then one might conclude that contemporary theory is not much farther along toward a new articulation of ideology theory than Althusser was in the late 1960s. On the other hand, finally admitting the intractability of the grammatical subject might compel those of us in composition to theorize differently than we have. It might compel us to theorize the "instrument" of writing as being the very site of writing subject-formation.

Ideology in Rhetoric

To this point, comprehensive or ontological theories of *rhetoric* and *ideology* have not been made to coexist in one theoretical formulation. And perhaps they can't. Berlin's tactic of subordination, whereby rhetoric is subsumed under ideology, may be necessary to a theory that sought to establish *ideology* as the ontological ground of composition. To instead give *rhetoric* such pride of place is, in a way, to resist ideology, if one agrees with Paolo Valesio that ideology is actually "decayed rhetoric—rhetoric that is no longer the detailed expression of strategies at work in specific discourses" (66). In Berlin's work, the elevation of ideology theory happens at the expense of rhetorical theory, as rhetoric is identified in this scheme as merely the distributor of hegemonic goods. In order for this subordination to work—that is, to cohere theoretically—ontological theories of rhetoric (such as Paolo Valesio's) must be ignored and, more importantly, future ontological theories of rhetoric must be foreclosed. In chapter 5, I will argue that such a foreclosure is a good idea, albeit for different reasons. But for the moment, we can bring this matter back to composition's object of study by noting, as Baudrillard does in *The Perfect Crime*, that theories of ideology (such as Berlin's) simply ignore the (f)act of writing:

> Ideological and moralistic critique, obsessed with meaning and content, obsessed with the political finality of discourse, never takes into account writing, the act of writing, the poetic, ironic, allusive force of language, of the juggling with meaning. It does not see that the resolution of meaning is to be found there—in the form itself, the formal materiality of expression. (*Perfect* 103)

To put it still another way: ontological ideology theory, obsessed with a hermeneutic vision of being, will not be able to understand a nonrepresentationalist theory of writing.

Berlin's work assumes that writing carries ideological meaning, and it focuses on the need to discern that meaning and to speculate on the ways such meaning gets inserted into writing. By doing so, his work articulates a writing subject that is an *interpreting subject*, one that participates—when in the writing class—in what Bruce McComiskey calls "production criticism," a process whereby students "gain a solid understanding of how texts produce certain social meanings" but "are not encouraged to formulate particular critical stances toward (or subject positions in relation to) the key terms, oppositions, and narratives they find represented in social institutions and cultural artifacts" (23). In such a scheme, writing can only come in two forms. First, it is the already completed text, often but not exclusively graphic, which, as a carrier of meaning, is to be "read" by the interpreting subject. Second, writing is the activity by which the interpreting subject generates the results of its search for meanings within the first form. Just as the "read" text carries meaning to be discerned by the interpreting subject, so the "written" text carries meaning to be discerned by another interpreting subject, the writing teacher, thus transforming that "written" text instantly into another "read" text. The infinite regress of reading in search of ever-elusive meaning is underway.

But I am suggesting a more theoretically tenable way to arrange this constellation of subjects, actions, and objects, one requiring theorists to adhere to two distinct yet complementary positions. First is the understanding that to write is to act on a kind of faith, to act on the belief that "meaning" will issue at the supposed end of a signification process (e.g., when one's work is read). This requires, of course, a corresponding belief in the end of signification, in a result of writing that is something other than more of itself. To write is to expect to realize values located outside of writing—values such as the solving of a problem, the expression of an emotion, the achievement of justice, or the conveying of an idea. Perhaps writing subjects must believe writing to be a meaning-full activity in order for them to do it. The second, simultaneous position for theorists is the understanding that the end of signification never happens, that there is no end of writing, no payoff of meaning or value that is not itself writing. This is the understanding that the belief enabling writing is just that, a belief. It is not a logical or rational assumption or conclusion.

Writing theorized in this way involves first a necessary misrecognition, in this case the belief that one is effecting meaning (i.e., attaching the descriptive figures of the symbolic order to their described counterparts in reality) rather than manipulating form (i.e., arranging descriptive figures of the symbolic order in relation to each other). But it also involves the recognition of this misrecognition. To hold both is to understand, following Slavoj Žižek, that ideology works at the level of doing rather than knowing (30–33). For compositionists, it is to understand that ideology is not found in some supposedly latent content of writing but rather as a function of the act of writing itself. To sit before a blank screen or empty notepad and begin the process of arranging graphic symbols is already to have begun acting ideologically, regardless of what the text, the artifact that will in retrospect be called a "piece of writing," might "say." Theorized in this way, ideology and writing both occur on the discursive surface, not in the epistemic depths.

This theorization insists, then, on a general theory of the surface. This general theory is the description of the means by which the action of ideology takes place. But any theory of the surface is bound to be a part of that surface, and so not a theory as such, but more surface features. It is just another figuration of the symbolic order. Or, to invoke yet another familiar term, it is caught in the play of difference. But if writing is the act of arranging the graphic figures of the symbolic (as I am doing now, or, as I will have been doing when you read this) in an act of believing/pretending to "mean," then to study writing might be to try to explain why and how it is that when one writes, one acts as if meaning were to issue. That it never does issue, because the arrangement of symbols (or, signifiers) is only ever "understood" through the further arrangement of symbols, is something else that the study of writing might try always to account for.

And what of the writing subject? If ideology is realized in the act of writing rather than in its hoped-for effects at a particular point in time, what can be said of "the one" who effects this graphic, symbolic arrangement? I will address this question in detail in the final chapter. But for the moment, one way to think about the writing subject might be to say that the space of agency to which one assigns the name "writer" is necessarily elusive, not available to direct empirical observation or to rationalist theorization. That is, "the writer" is always identified after the (f)act, after textual remnants have turned up, even when empirical observation—for example, through ethnography—is carried out on "the writer" in the act itself. These textual remnants— pieces of writing, field notes—serve as the evidence that an act of writing took place, that an action—writing—was carried about by an agent, a writing subject. At first glance, such an observation seems to reiterate the issues laid out by Derrida in "Signature Event Context," where time is used as a wedge to pry open the black box of writing, which contains writing's secret, which is that it does not "communicate" "ideas." But as I indicated in chapter 1, our theoretical explanations of writing remain situated in the late 1960s and 1970s, as do our theories of ideology.

The difference—or at least, the difference for composition theory—is that unlike philosophy or theory as understood in other areas of English studies, composition theorizes the act of writing in the belief that interventions in this unavailable (unobservable, untheorizable) act can and must be made. In other words, composition is interested in *improving* writing processes and products, whatever that might mean at a given time. So it must assume the presence of, on the one hand, an empirically identifiable act and, on the other hand, a pedagogically available subject that performs this act. Composition, like writers, proceeds on faith, in the belief that writing is the production of meaning, and in the belief that the writing subject controls this production. But it must also renounce that faith, as I have been suggesting here, in order to more accurately explain the (f)act of writing.

And ideology theory plays a part in this explanation. Despite its theoretical problems, it is still possible to say that an appropriately attenuated "ideology," understood as action or practice, could be of use toward a theory of writing. I have tried to show how ideology theory has mistakenly been used to explain writing rather than the other way around. Thus, discussions of "rhetoric *and* ideology in the writing class" have been discussions of rhetoric *in* ideology. By going back to Althusser and highlighting theoretical problems in ideology theory itself, I have tried to show how and why this subordination of rhetoric to ideology is a consequence of those prior problems. In the discourse of ideology of which Althusser is the source, ideology's comprehensive, ontological status is almost axiomatic. Only its particular dimensions and contours are fruitfully debated. Yet Althusser himself seems to argue against this position, particularly when the question of agency arises. My claim, that "ideology" is one of the many terminological residues of writing rather than a master *concept* explaining all features of existence, might help composition theorists better conduct future investigations.

✤4✤

Theories of Culture
in Composition Theory

Cultural theory of one kind or another has been a valuable resource for composition theory. But it has tended to arrive by way of literary studies. That is, it has been understood by composition theorists as a powerful tool for analyzing and interpreting texts rather than as a potential means by which to theorize writing itself. This means that while versions of composition theory influenced by cultural studies have made new inquiries possible, for the most part they have not addressed central theoretical issues. In this chapter, I examine some theoretical and pedagogical consequences of composition theory's appropriation of cultural theory. First, I look briefly at two composition textbooks, several pedagogical articles, and one example of cultural/composition theory itself in order to highlight the hermeneutic—and therefore narrowly representational—theory of writing that such approaches authorize.

Then, I offer readings of several now-canonical texts in composition studies, arguing that, taken as a group, they plot a historical and conceptual trajectory of the writing subject which the rest of the field has overlooked. Finally, I argue that the next step in this trajectory of the writing subject has yet to be taken, and that it is precisely here where a theory of culture and a theory of writing can be brought together in order to describe the act of writing not as representation technology but as the production of reproduction. I will put into conversation the nonrepresentational, non-hermeneutic theory of writing toward which this project has been working and two different but related examples of cultural theory that make theoretical arguments similar to my own. Specifically, Homi Bhabha's "The Postcolonial and the Postmodern: The Question of Agency" and Gayatri Spivak's "Subaltern Studies: Deconstructing Historiography" break with the hermeneutic paradigm that informs so much of literary studies, cultural studies, and composition studies. Thus, I bring them into this discussion not for their theoretical insights as such, but for the ways they bring those insights to bear on topics—culture and writing, respectively—that are of crucial importance to composition theory. The writing subject evoked through such an operation is quite different than the one articulated by composition theory to date. But it is not a departure. We have been moving in this direction for some time.

Hermeneutic Imperialism

While the work of traditional English studies remains the teaching of textual interpretation, the work of composition has been the teaching of textual production. As my examples in this chapter will indicate, recent composition theory resembles literary theory in its attention to textual interpretation. But it does not theorize textual action, except insofar as it rationalizes interpretation as a form of action. In other words, it uses cultural theory much as the rest of English does: as an approach by which to decode or unpack existing texts. Susan Miller laments the emergence of this hermeneutic perspective in composition and calls instead for a rhetorical perspective, one whereby "acts of writing, not interpreted texts . . . warrant analysis by humanists interested in revealing the texture of a culture" (*Assuming* 4). I will follow up on this call by suggesting that such a perspective can be adopted if one understands that neither culture nor writing should be mistaken for the particlar artifacts they leave behind. Nor should these artifacts be thought to contain "within" them something of the essence of either. To do so is to commit oneself to a fundamentally hermeneutic disposition, one that will yield answers recognizable only within a hermeneutic framework. According to John Guillory, literary study is in crisis because it offers students "a form of capital increasingly marginal to the social function of the present educational system" (x). The habits of mind first associated with the study of canonical literature no longer serve a widespread cultural purpose. Yet that field seems only dimly aware of its own cultural history and of how that history relates to its current problems. In terms of curriculum and disciplinarity, literary study has become, Guillory notes, "a specialization among many others," but it has not let go of its "*universalist* rationale" (264). This rationale is the remnant of a time when the literacy that English departments promoted was a cultural common denominator required of an emerging class of people passing through the university for the first time (264).

For the most part, cultural theory in English studies has been part of an attempt allow that field to keep its old universalist rationale by offering cultural capital that might appeal to a broader constituency than that of the traditional English major. In the past, English conferred its capital through a relatively limited set of newly canonized literary texts, along with a method by which to read them. With cultural theory, which offers a broad range of interpretable texts, English tries to confer capital by promoting a general interpretive savvy, a hermeneutic dexterity with "texts" of all kinds. But cultural theory can also complicate the question of interpretation through its interest in the sociological and the material. This complication allows English to assert that it trains people to become astute "readers" of their text-saturated, sign-saturated surroundings in order to become better cultural analysts. This claim, in turn, allows English to bid for conceptual and political centrality in the humanities. But, as Guillory suggests and as Sharon Crowley's *Composition in the University* shows, English has long asserted its centrality, implicitly and otherwise. In this current episode, it has simply used cultural theory to try to regain position.

Ironically, the precedent for English studies' appropriation of cultural theory can be found in its prior appropriation of rhetoric. From Wayne Booth to Steven Mailloux, literary theorists have argued for the importance of rhetoric to textual interpretation. As with cultural theory, English has chosen those aspects of rhetoric most adaptable to its hermeneutic project while avoiding others.[1] Compositionists interested both in cultural and rhetorical theory must be able to distinguish between those aspects of each attending to textual production—the aspects often left out of literary accounts of these fields—and those that do not. As composition struggles to become more theoretically sophisticated by claiming cultural and rhetorical theory as legitimate intellectual resources, it needs to reckon with English studies' power to reproduce both in its own image. Thus far, evidence indicates that composition has been unable to do so. We can see examples of this reproduction even in such an important book as James Berlin's *Rhetorics, Poetics, and Cultures*, which seeks to reconstitute English studies as a rhetorical field of inquiry. As Miller has noted, this book understands rhetoric mainly as hermeneutic, and it therefore understands the writing class as preparation for (and practice in) cultural decoding ("Technologies" 499). In other words, while the subject matter of Berlin's version of English studies significantly increases (thanks to the influence of cultural theory), and while the critical tools Berlin brings to bear on that subject matter are likewise much more sophisticated, the work remains the same: students interpret texts.

Cultural Theory in a Composition Textbook

This feature of Berlin's work occurs elsewhere in the field, and fairly often, especially in pedagogical discussions. Cultural theory influences composition studies' idea of the appropriate subject matter about which students should write, as well as, on occasion, the analytical tools they should bring to bear on it. But cultural theory has little if any influence on the field's conception of writing itself. This fact reflects a failure of composition theory, one that has had wide impact.

One area of impact is the composition textbook industry, which I want briefly to examine by pointing to a textbook informed by cultural theory in the ways I have just described. *Seeing & Writing 2*, by Donald McQuade and Christine McQuade, is the second edition of a book that is considered to be groundbreaking in its emphasis on visual texts as subject matter for student writing. Yet for all its innovation in this area, both editions of the book present writing in narrow and traditional ways that demonstrate no consideration of cultural theory and its impact on theories of writing. Specifically, the book presents writing in a very familiar way: as a technology to be put in the service of hermeneutic activity. I take the fact that such textbooks exist—and I want to be clear that *Seeing & Writing* is not unique or especially blameworthy in this regard; it is merely one example—as evidence that composition theory has failed composition studies by not offering new theoretical models for how to imagine, study, or teach writing.

Seeing & Writing explains to students that they will "learn, recognize, understand, and create compelling and convincing messages that will be understood by many people" by learning "the skills identified with both verbal and visual literacy" (xxxii). Yet while the book offers detailed and theoretically sophisticated instructions on how to read or *see* texts, its advice on how to *write* texts is brief and arhetorical. Students are told that writers "usually start by searching for and then deciding on a subject to write about, developing their ideas about the subject, clarifying their purpose in writing, organizing their thoughts, and considering the audience they want to address" (xlvi). The key assumptions here, as with other composition textbooks, are that writing occurs mainly in response to a school assignment and that everyone involved understands the details of that particular rhetorical situation. *Seeing & Writing* positions its primary readers as students whose rhetorical task is to satisfy a writing instructor, and who already know the set of conventions by which to effect that satisfaction. The book also imagines a writing instructor who expects students to fulfill the assignment without explicit instruction in how to compose.

In subsequent chapters, the apparatus devoted to writing instruction repeatedly asks students to "write an essay" on the topic at hand. But the book does not treat the essay as a genre with a history and a range of rhetorical purposes, and it does not show students how actually to write one. The book gives students many occasions to write, but it gives them little instruction in how to do it. Having been shown the fundamentals of the writing process in a brief introductory chapter, students are expected to apply that information to their presumably preexisting knowledge of conventions. The problem with this approach, as Mina Shaughnessy and David Bartholomae demonstrated years go, is that first year college students do not necessarily have that genre knowledge. For students who are not white and/or middle-class, especially, this kind of assignment can be at best a puzzle, at worst a threat. By enacting the theoretical mistake of converting hermeneutics from a technical skill into a way of being, *Seeing & Writing* upholds, as do many composition textbooks, the representationalist paradigm of writing. And, in doing so, it helps preserve educational inequality by keeping the writing process essentially mysterious. An increased sensitivity to the very idea of culture may have influenced the selection of texts and topics about which students in composition classes are made to write, but this case and others indicate that it has had no effect on anyone's understanding of writing. *Seeing & Writing*, and many other less ambitious textbooks, remain firmly traditional in their pedagogy and narrowly representational in their theory.

If it is the case, as Bob Connors has argued, that composition textbooks teach composition instructors as much as they teach students, then it is little wonder that the representationalist ideology of writing has so firm a grip on composition studies. Not much is happening at the theory end of the field to suggest to researchers that writing should be conceived of otherwise, and textbooks, which circulate widely among both specialists and nonspecialists, "teach" new instructors in the old and familiar ways, even when they are informed by some form or another of cultural theory.

Cultural Theory in the Composition Curriculum

In the early 1990s, there were some opportunities to develop a cultural theory of writing, that is, a conception of writing that fully and carefully explained its role in the production and formation of culture. But this would have involved stepping away from the hermeneutic paradigm, which consigns writing to the role of representational technology. Instead, in the early 1990s, the literary studies version of cultural theory appeared in composition studies, specifically in pedagogical articles describing classroom practice and curriculum. James Berlin and Michael Vivion's classic collection, *Cultural Studies in the English Classroom*, offers several examples.

In "One Person, Many Worlds: A Multi-Cultural Composition Curriculum," Deloris Schriner describes a course built on the proposition that all students experience "multi-cultural social realities" (98). In the series of writing assignments that comprises this course, students are asked to "consider notions of individuality and the ways that individuals control and direct their experiences"; to "consider the social and cultural factors which also work to control and direct experiences"; and to "reflect on the intersections between individuality and society" (98–99). The purpose of the assignments is "to foster critical thinking and the development of interpretive abilities" (99). These assignments come in two basic forms, the "personal writing assignment" and the "reading assignment." In the former, students demonstrate their ability to "reflect," "think," and "consider" while mining their past experiences for topics. In the latter, they "focus," "describe," "look," and, again, "consider" in response to particular readings. At no point, it seems, are students given instruction about how to carry out these assignments. Nor do they discuss the generic forms and rhetorical purposes of the texts they are asked to produce. In other words, writing is not a theorized activity in this course. Instead, the course uses writing to do other work, notably to teach reflection and interpretation, but the act of writing itself is neither understood nor presented to students as a participatory, cultural, rhetorical act. Of course, the absence of an explicit theory of writing does not mean that no theory of writing is present. There is an implicit theory here, and it is the same one that underwrites the writing done in most literature courses: that writing is a device by which a nondiscursive subject conveys "thoughts" or similarly interiorized constructs. There is also an implicit genre here: the personal/literary essay. But the assumption, as in most literature courses, is that the student is already familiar with the genre. Cultural studies, in this case, is being used to theorize the complexities of reading, but the corresponding complexities of writing are not addressed.

Likewise, Lori Robison's " 'This Could Have Been Me': Composition and the Implications of Cultural Perspective" describes a composition course that aims to teach students to interpret texts and offer written evidence of that skill. For Robison, "finding ways to demonstrate to students that writing can be closely connected to the world outside of the classroom" is a difficult and important task (233). Unfortunately, Robison's only strategy for establishing those connections is to have students "consider" and "reflect" upon "their own cultural situation" in order to "make meaning" (233). In other words, the student's relationship to the world is that of a reader to a text. Robison does note the importance of writing oneself into a variety of perspectives. She identifies writing "as a process of placing and locating the self within a culture" (233), but her assignments indicate that this process derives from an essentially reflective and interpretive act which, however engaged and alert and provisional, is nonetheless an act of reception, not production. The texts Robison's students write are like literary explications. And, as instances of student writing, they exist to be evaluated, serving as the documentary remnant of a thought process. They are the same in kind as the texts produced through literary training in traditional English studies.

Robison's first major assignment asks students to "reconsider" the sources from which they had developed a preliminary sense of their topic, the 1960s, "in order to consider what it means to study or define an historical period" through traditional sources (236). Later, after conducting group research projects that encourage them to find traditional and nontraditional sources, Robison asks students "to reflect on this process of coming to an interpretation of another historical period" so that they may "consider how we come to terms with the past from our own cultural and historical perspective" (236). For the final project, Robison asks students to write a paper "in which they [develop] their own explanation for today's interest in the 1960s through an interpretation of the cultural representations we [have] examined together as a class" (237).

Robison writes that the course was a success, in part because "many of the students seemed to have found ways to make their writing matter; they wrote papers that suggested that they had explored issues and discovered concerns of profound social and personal importance" (237). But beyond developing their interpretive skills and practicing them on a variety of nontraditional texts, it is not clear how the training students received here is different from that offered in a very good, theoretically informed literature course. In other words, like a literature course, this composition course offers students the opportunity and equipment to interpret texts in new and potentially radical ways, particularly when it encourages "readings" of nonliterary texts. But in this scenario writing is, once again, only a means to an end, the by-product of a prior, interpretive act. It is not imagined or understood by the instructor as a cultural and rhetorical activity in its own right. Nor is it presented to the students as such. There is of course an implicit rhetoric being enacted here, but it is the rhetoric of literary interpretation.

Once again, we can trace what happens in such articles to the failure of composition theory to offer a theory of writing beyond the literary/hermeneutic paradigm. It could be said that composition theory has hardly even approached its own objects of study, the act of writing and the writing subject, for years. We read potentially informative discourses, such as cultural studies and postcolonial theory, according to the rubric of literary studies. Our theory having, in effect, avoided the implications of cultural theory for writing, composition studies has no cultural theory of writing, at least not one that is widespread.

Cultural Theory in Composition Theory

One particularly unfortunate aspect of composition theory's avoidance of cultural theory has been the missed opportunity to address the question of "the subject." After all, cultural theory's concern with the subject echoes composition's concern with the writing subject as articulated in some of the field's most significant works. For that matter, the act of writing is often a stated concern of cultural theorists. In fact, certain expressions of it treat writing as a culturally and politically significant mode of production. For example, Edward Said's *Orientalism* identifies administrative, academic, and creative writing as crucial vehicles for the construction and dissemination of a dominant ideology. In *Writing Diaspora*, Rey Chow addresses what she calls "the tactics of dealing with and dealing in dominant cultures" carried out in, among other venues, literary productions (25).

Using cultural studies as a framework, James Berlin's *Rhetorics, Poetics, and Cultures* begins to theorize writing culturally. But as I noted above, its theoretical orientation assumes and invokes subjects characterized more by their interpretation of signs than their production of them. That is, they read more than they write, and their writing is often only meant to serve as evidence of their reading. In this way, Berlin's work participates in what Dilip Gaonkar calls the "contemporary impulse to universalize rhetoric" by making it a "hermeneutic metadiscourse" (26, 25). Rather than take this hermeneutic approach to writing, composition theory should examine the acts of control, resistance, adaptation, and accommodation that composing subjects, who are both producers and products of discourse, carry out. More importantly, it might attend to and explore nonrepresentational functions of writing, functions that would situate writing more deeply in the matrix of cultural (re)production than current perspectives have been able to. That is, if one were to fuse composition theory's interest in understanding writing to cultural theory's concern with explaining how ideological formulations are rooted in uneven power relations, one would prepare the ground for empirical studies that might, in time, provide a more comprehensive accounf of writing *as*, rather than *in*, culture.

Since the late 1960s, composition theory has been concerned with the construction of written texts because its pedagogical mission has been fairly clear: to help people write effectively, whatever "effectively" might mean at a given moment. But if the above example is any indication, cultural theory would seem to be of little use to composition theory in the same way that much postmodern theory is of little use: neither tends to recognize—much less theorize—the composing processes that produce the texts whose meanings and effects they so carefully analyze. Despite this, I believe that composition theory should address cultural theory's analyses of discourse practices and effects in order to better articulate its own theoretical (and cultural) understandings of writing. Until it has done so, composition studies will be unable to theorize writing fully as cultural (re)production, that is, as the production of the conditions for representation, conditions whereby such terms as "culture" come to be understood as having various "meanings."

I noted above that cultural theory and composition theory share a concern for "the subject." In composition theory, the most notable example of this concern is Susan Miller's 1989 book, *Rescuing the Subject*, which argues for a "differently modeled writer, who is not the author," and who "has a relation to texts that never exceeds, but that also must fall within, a greater field of concerns than those we are accustomed to accounting for in our equations of a text's possible significance with its 'meaning'" (14). While the question of the subject in composition precedes Miller's explicit theorization, the disciplinary narratives we devise for ourselves and our graduate students often fail to tell this story in this way. In what follows, I will examine some key texts in composition theory to highlight the subject—the writing subject—that our field has articulated over time. Then I will show how the new subjects articulated in Spivak's and Bhabha's works point the way for composition theorists to continue developing theories of the writing subject. As a composition theorist, I am interested in theorizing writers and writing in order to account for the increasingly networked world into which both emerge. I am also interested in theoretical explanations of how the act of writing functions in contexts that can be described broadly as cultural. Globalization and the proliferation of technology make it imperative that compositionists develop a new kind of composition theory, one that understands its object of study very broadly and is conscious of its methodologies. If we understand culture and writing in temporal terms, as do Bhabha and Spivak to some extent, then we take a first step in that direction. But as I noted, the story of the cultural subject has been underway for some time in composition studies, specifically in the development of the writing subject.

In different ways, the work of Janet Emig, Mina Shaughnessy, David Bartholomae, and Miller has offered new ways of seeing writers—in particular, student writers—as subjects situated within, defined by, and sometimes moving across discourses. These theorizations, among others, mark composition's principal contribution to what has been called "the linguistic turn" in the humanities and beyond. Implicitly at times, explicitly at others, these compositionists show us that makers of texts are themselves components of both prior and ongoing textualities. The making of texts, therefore, is an extraordinarily complex act that merits close and rigorous study.

At this late date, it might seem that such observations about the history of research composition need no longer be made.

The attention to language, at least in literary and critical theory, might lead one to think that others now understand the interpretation of texts to be but one aspect of textual analysis. But this is not the case. For example, there are few intradisciplinary conversations between composition theorists and their counterparts in other areas of textual study. Few people outside of composition studies refer to the work of composition theorists to further their own arguments or to extend the range of knowledge in their fields. More importantly, few people outside of composition have begun asking significantly different questions of the texts they study, questions that compositionists have asked for three decades. While scholars outside of composition studies tend to ask what texts mean, researchers in composition studies tend to ask what is involved in making meaningful texts. Because of this profound difference, it is useful, especially for those new to the field, to understand clearly composition theory's contribution to composition studies up to the early 1990s. Moreover, it is important to understand how the field's past research—regardless of its particular methodology or theoretical approach—can be used to set the terms of discussion in contemporary and future composition theory.[2]

For example, it is probably commonplace in graduate composition theory courses to discuss Emig's *The Composing Processes of Twelfth Graders* in terms of the *writing process* it helped codify. But I suspect that it is less common in such classes to discuss what I see as that book's more substantive and enduring contribution, which is the invention of a "writing subject." Emig places writers and the act of writing—not texts nor readers—at the center of attention and analysis. She does this on the then-bold assumption that knowledge about writing itself is to be gained by studying ongoing processes rather than finished products. Of course, *The Composing Processes of Twelfth Graders* does not *explicitly* put forth a new theory of the writing subject. Rather, the book simply enacts one, assuming the very idea of such a subject existing at all, asserting that writers and acts of writing should be empirically observed and subsequently explained. Emig herself describes the study's "chief value" to be "its steady assumption that persons, rather than mechanisms, compose" (5). Here, she is specifically referring to dry and rigid pedagogies that teach writing as a linear movement from a thought to its printed expression, and she is suggesting instead that effective pedagogies will only arise from a greater understanding of what people actually do when they sit down to write. To do so requires the creation of a conceptual space, which I am calling, after Foucault, the writing subject, that had not previously been acknowledged ("What is an Author?" 102). Furthermore, the implications of her study are broader than usually imagined. If writing happens as a recursive, nonlinear process, then it cannot be said to represent thought in any direct way because it actually plays a role in the *development* of thought. So, in Emig's work, a writing subject is conjured for perhaps the first time, and a new discourse begins to emerge by which to address the very nature and functions of writing.

It is easy to understand how such a new subject—a writing subject—would seem foreign to those whose attention is devoted to already written and highly valued texts that ostensibly convey the thoughts and sentiments of an individual. Beyond the influence of literary studies' theoretical and methodological hegemony, Emig suggests that analytical emphasis can and should be placed on the producers of texts, not on the texts themselves nor on their real or idealized receivers. By not fetishizing the text and the reader, Emig's assertion becomes the theoretical and methodological foundation of the field, the feature that will begin to distinguish composition studies from the rest of English studies.

Despite Emig's revolutionary and influential decision to focus on writing processes rather than writing products, Shaughnessy's *Errors and Expectations* returns to the latter. Shaughnessy performs on student writing the kinds of analyses and interpretations that literary scholars might recognize. But unlike literary interpretations, which construct an ideal act of reading by establishing meanings that represent a text's fulfilled intentions, Shaughnessy's interpretations have different goals and achieve very different results. They reconstruct the act of writing embodied in those texts, positing a writer's unfulfilled intentions. Unlike literary texts, the texts she analyzes do not "work"; they fail to mean what their writers intend. Yet their failure is systematic, not chaotic, as many unprepared teachers encountering "basic writing" for the first time had reasonably believed. Shaughnessy showed that students' texts contain evidence of a systematic, if flawed, process. This process is enacted by a particular writing subject, the "basic writer." This is a unique and rich theoretical contribution to an English studies which, at the time of *Errors'* publication in 1977, was itself coming to terms with other theoretical complexities regarding to the text (i.e., deconstruction) and its reception (i.e., reader-response theory). The considerable research into writing and writing processes that Shaughnessy made possible need not be rehearsed here. But it is important to remember that she and the many who worked in her wake created a new field of inquiry (i.e., basic writing) with a new object of study (basic writers) at about the same time that the phenomenon of "theory" itself was beginning to force literary studies to reconceptualize the ontological status of its own traditional object of study. Furthermore, while Shaughnessy's examinations of student writing may have been informed by a relatively narrow method of analysis, the results she obtained reach far beyond literature or the basic writing classroom. As Susan Miller has argued, the detailed understandings that Shaughnessy's analysis made possible revealed the historical constructedness of *all* textual stances, not just those of the basic writer (*Rescuing* 166). In other words, Shaughnessy's analysis begins to theorize the position of the writing subject *as* a subject position, one recognized, if not exactly understood, by literary studies. And this occurs at approximately the same time that literary studies begins to theorize the reader of literature *as* a subject position. Composition theory and literary theory thus direct attention away from the textual artifact and toward, respectively, its production and reception.[3]

These theoretical dimensions of Shaughnessy's work are subsequently made explicit by David Bartholomae, whose work marks another point on the theoretical trajectory toward a fully realized theory of the writing subject. Bartholomae's "Inventing the University" is informed by both Shaughnessy and Michel Foucault. Its close and careful readings continue Shaughnessy's tradition of giving the same care to student texts that literature teachers give to canonical texts. But, following Foucault, Bartholomae extends this idea by theorizing the relationship between writers and the university exhorting them to adopt the subject position of student-writer. Bartholomae shows that writers with limited exposure to the discourse conventions and subject matters of the university make texts that try to disguise this lack of knowledge. More importantly, he shows that the institution actually encourages students to do this. In fact, he argues that most people acquire knowledge precisely through such acts of approximation, especially in the early stages of a course of study. Foucault's theorizing of both institutional power and the circulation of discourse make it possible for Bartholomae to identify and articulate a relationship between the individual and the university, between student and teacher—a relationship conducted largely through written texts and acts of writing—in ways that previous composition theories had not. In turn, new theories and pedagogies emerge that reflect an understanding of writing as a fundamentally social activity, one connected to a larger network of significations than those accounted for by the prevailing cognitive theories of the day.

While Bartholomae's work articulates a theory of the writing subject, this theory is not realized until the publication of Miller's *Rescuing the Subject.* Miller's book explains why the classical model of the "good man speaking well" is inadequate to the task of describing or explaining the writer and the act of writing in postmodern or even modern circumstances. According to Miller, "writing constructs a subject quite different from the unitary speaking subject whom both modern philosophy and oral rhetoric have imagined" (4). She offers a historical analysis of how theories of language and rhetoric have groped toward this realization, and of how historical changes in the conditions and purposes of writing made the field of composition "an inevitable cultural outcome"

(2). *Rescuing the Subject* opens the way for further investigation, both theoretical and empirical, of what current and future acts of writing will require of writers and readers. This new theory of the writer—of the writing subject—is based on what Miller calls *textual rhetoric*, a theory of discourse by which it is possible "to investigate the human 'writer' without necessarily surrounding that person with the now easily deniable claptrap of inspired, unitary 'authorship' that contemporary theorists in other fields have so thoroughly deconstructed" (3). Ironically, the implications of Miller's book were largely ignored in the 1990s as composition theory turned away from writing en route to its misappropriation of cultural theory, which I have already discussed.

Cultural Theory and Writing Theory

It is possible, even necessary, to theorize writing and culture together. In order to do so, composition theorists need to approach cultural theory not as a set of ideas to be applied or adapted, but as a discourse that overlaps with composition theory at certain points of mutual interest. It is not a question of importing "foreign" theories to lend disciplinary prestige or intellectual heft to composition studies. Rather, it is a question of using any and all means available to come up with better descriptions of our objects of study: writing and writing subjects. To this point, cultural composition theory has asserted that written language is situated within complex cultural systems, and in doing so it has retained the narrow, representationalist theory of writing. That is, using existing cultural theory, composition theory has asserted the importance of writing owing to its perceived location near the core of cultural signification. But while this claim has positioned writing in the service of *something else* called culture, it has said nothing new about writing itself. In this formulation, writing is once more a form of representation. Specifically, it is a representation technology, and culture is the content represented through it. This does not amount to a better description of the field's objects of study. Rather, it takes the same descriptions and puts them in different contexts.

So, again, the challenge for composition theorists is to theorize writing. And if it appears that certain theories of culture overlap with certain accounts of writing when both try to explain the relationship between culture and textuality, then it is worth the composition theorist's effort to see if this overlap can itself generate any new insights that might not have been arrived at otherwise. I argue that this is the case with Bhabha's "The Postcolonial and the Postmodern." In its refusal to theorize culture as that which is *contained* (in artifacts, practices, or even ideas), Bhabha's argument complements my case against theorizing writing as *container* (of anything), or representation technology. Specifically, Bhabha's argument undercuts the notion that culture is *something else* represented in, for example, writing. Instead, it recasts culture as the name for one effect or function of various acts of production, including writing.

Bhabha describes this theoretical relocation of culture as a way to "[bear] witness to the unequal and uneven forces of cultural representation involved in the contest for political and social authority within the modern world order" (171). He examines various forms of cultural production arising from the places where cultures mingle and clash. For Bhabha, the postcolonial postmodern theorist must "confront the concept of culture outside *objets d'art* or beyond the canonization of the 'idea' of aesthetics, to engage with culture as an uneven, incomplete production of meaning and value, often composed of incommensurable demands and practices, produced in the act of social survival" (172). Examinations of the aesthetic are valuable and necessary; they call attention to the political dimensions of art, particularly when conditions of inequity and subjugation are documented in aesthetic forms; they show how artistic production participates in the social, cultural, and political life of specific groups of people. But the potentially powerful cultural analytic of cultural theory should also be a way to investigate beyond the aesthetic, and at times it is. Still, the resilience of a narrow version of textuality, despite the influx of new and potentially radical theories of textuality, underscores the hegemonic power of English studies' ability to absorb difference.

At any rate, in attempting to relocate culture by renaming "the postmodern from the position of the postcolonial," Bhabha identifies two analytical orientations, derived from Foucault, from which the issue of culture can be approached.[4] He calls these "the epistemological" and "the enunciative" (175). In the former, cultural incommensurability is absorbed into an overarching conceptual scheme that attempts to arrive at "holistic forms of social explanation" (173). In the latter, questions of temporality, location, and acts of articulation occupy the conceptual foreground. Incommensurability is examined according to these terms, but it is not absorbed into a larger conceptual system. Bhabha pursues this difference at length:

> If culture as epistemology focuses on function and intention, then culture as enunciation focuses on signification and institutionalization; if the epistemological tends towards a *reflection* of its empirical referent or object, the enunciative attempts repeatedly to reinscribe and relocate the political claim to cultural priority . . . in the social institution of the signifying activity. The epistemological is locked into the hermeneutic circle, in the description of cultural elements as they tend towards a totality. The enunciative is a more dialogic process that attempts to track displacements and realignments that are the effects of cultural antagonisms and articulations—subverting the rationale of the hegemonic moment and relocating alternative, hybrid sites of cultural negotiation. (177–78)

Culture-as-enunciation treats acts and places rather than things and ideas. It attends to the discursive and the temporal event, to the (f)act of production rather than the implications of representation. Culture is produced by partisans; it is the process of interaction, persuasion, and coercion rather than a reflection of the abstract and atemporal. The "displacements and realignments that are the effects of cultural antagonisms and articulations" recall the activities that Kenneth Burke, in more homespun terms, referred to as "the flurries and flare-ups of the Human Barnyard" (23). To "reinscribe and relocate" is to invent and arrange, though not necessarily at the merely individual level. In these ways, Bhabha's approach to cultural production is significantly different than that of other cultural theorists. Enunciation is the contest over commonplaces, the struggle for control over the "means of production." The location of culture is the signifying activity itself, not the signifiers nor the things they are supposed to carry.

This framework complicates the question of agency, or of the subject, which has always been at the center of composition studies. Without some notion of agency, without a subject, however implicit, composition as a field of inquiry would seem to lose its intellectual purpose. Yet my narrative of the writing subject's progress from Emig to Miller argues that not much has happened since 1989, so it is time revisit the question, as I will do here and in the next chapter.

If we agree with Bhabha that culture is enunciation, then we can argue that writing—a form of enunciation—does not merely record cultural contexts. Instead, we can argue that writing creates cultural contexts. Specifically, the act of writing is the (re)creating of cultural contexts. Writing is not the graphic evidence, nor the notation technology, of a culture's ideas or sentiments. It is the mechanism for producing statements that will, after the (f)act, be named "ideas" and "sentiments." For Bhabha, establishing culture-as-enunciation is a first step toward "a process by which objectified others may be turned into subjects of their history and experience" (becoming, in effect, writers) rather than remain the objects of someone else's history and experience (178). Cultural statements can be restated to the advantage of those who have, in his words, "suffered the sentence of history," those who have been disempowered by rhetorical strategies masquerading as inevitable results of history, philosophy, or science (172).

In light of the possibilities arising from Bhabha's argument, then, composition theorists might ask the following questions: How might cultural *re*statements occur specifically as written discourse? What kinds of writing subjects perform such acts? What is involved—materially, technically—in becoming the subject of one's history and experience? If culture is enunciation, and enunciation is a generalized way of describing writing, then culture is writing. If this is the case, then composition studies' previous ideas about the relation of writing to culture have been narrow and inaccurate. As with epistemology and ideology, culture is not represented or made manifest in writing. The act of writing and the subjects who perform it do not simply reflect this or that aspect of culture. Rather, because writing necessarily proceeds from a necessary misrecognition (as I argued in chapter 3), acts of writing produce exigencies that call for always-retrospective namings, which are themselves further instances of writing. The *something else* function or category which seems to be a structural component of writing is, at times, identified as "culture."

But again we find ourselves, as at the end of chapter 3, facing the question of the subject, trying to account for it within this general conception of writing. My narrative of the writing subject's birth and progress in composition studies stops with Miller's postmodern, textual subject. Yet the theory of writing for which I argue seems to require one more step in that progress.

Spivak's "Subaltern Studies: Deconstructing Historiography" begins to addresses one such writing subject by casting historiography as a rhetorical and political act of production. For Spivak, to write histories, especially revisionist histories, is to construct a past (and, by implication, a present) while in effect pretending necessarily to discover it. It is a strategy for making new stories that, in time and like the old stories, will no longer be considered stories at all. They will have passed into the meta-story known as History, Knowledge, or, in the following passage, Logic. Spivak writes:

What good does such an inscription do? It acknowledges that the arena of the subaltern's persistent emergence into hegemony must always and by definition
remain heterogeneous to the efforts of the disciplinary
historian. This historian must persist in *his* efforts in
this awareness that the subaltern is necessarily the
absolute limit of the place where history is narrativized
into logic. (217)

In other words, the subaltern historiographer writes the subaltern
subject into the discourse of History by buying into the otherwise
questionable concept of History. One *reports* and *analyzes* events
and people while realizing that one actually *renders* them. In the
specific case Spivak addresses, a group of radical historians establishes a new subaltern consciousness in the historical record
of British colonialism in India by reinterpreting archival material,
by "finding" what was "lost." Her later essay, "Can the Subaltern
Speak?" draws a clearer distinction between what Spivak calls
"the *mechanics* of the constitution" of subjects and "invocations
of the *authenticity*" of subjects (90). But in "Subaltern Studies,"
the invoking of authenticity is itself a mechanics of constitution.

The kind of writing Spivak describes here is an example of
what she calls, in other places, *strategic essentialism*. It has been
a contested notion for some time, and many have disagreed with
its effectiveness as a strategy. But the details of its practice are
distinct from the force of its theory and the example that it sets
for composition theorists. Spivak's essay argues that history and
culture are necessarily written, addressed practices. More importantly, it tries to offer a theory of the writing subject that coincides
with the impossibility of representation. Spivak's disciplinary historian necessarily proceeds as if historiography were possible
because historiography must be made to seem possible in order
to facilitate "the subaltern's persistent emergence into hegemony."
The subaltern cannot speak, and the historiographer cannot write,
but both do so anyway, the latter giving voice, as it were, to the
former. Actually, it is not so much that the historiographer cannot

write. It is that in the ongoing aftermath of writing, the term *history* can fill the *something else* requirement, as we might now expect. But, more importantly, the term *historiographer* can fill the *writing subject* requirement. Composition theory begins to mark the next step in the writing subject's progress when it redefines the writing subject not as a producer of writing but as a function of writing itself.

Of course, subaltern Indian historiography is just one context for the theoretical, textual maneuvers Spivak describes— perhaps a too exotic one. There are examples of such— "writtenness" in other areas. Those who study workplace writing, for example, and those who carry out ethnographic studies of writing communities are already engaged in a similar activity. But composition has yet to establish cultural theories of writing to help guide these studies, theories of cultural production that emphasize the act and processes of writing, and that situate the writing subject squarely within those acts and processes rather than alongside them. I have tried to link these statements by Bhabha and Spivak to composition's concerns by focusing on their attention to discourse production. In different ways, they understand writing as an impossibility which nevertheless happens. That is, they recognize the naivete involved in perceiving writing as merely representation, and they also understand the dogged persistence and perhaps intractabiity of that perception. Throughout this book, I have argued that composition theory should identify the representational paradigm, its presence at the core of the field's major theoretical assumptions, and its distorting effect on our understanding of writing. In the final chapter, I will examine the writing subject's role in the persistence of that paradigm and argue that, in fact, the next step in the writing subject's progress might be its dissolution.

❖5❖

Writing Without Subjects

Throughout this book, I have argued that composition theory since the early 1990s has described writing as little more than a technology of representation. Instead of offering different theoretical descriptions of writing, composition theory has inserted the old representationalist account of writing into various conceptual contexts such as those of epistemology, ideology, and culture. But these supposed concepts, I have argued, are better seen as particular effects of writing's apparently systemic function of invoking *something else*, which nonetheless and invariably turns out, upon examination, to be more writing. The most salient feature of writing is therefore not its representational function but its ability to proceed as if it has a representational function. For the most part, composition theory seems to have overlooked this difference, addressing the vagaries of specific issues within written representation rather than attempting to understand and explain the representation function that seems to be intrinsic to the system of writing.

In previous chapters, I have laid some of the blame for this situation at the doorstep of hermeneutics, specifically at our field's relatively uncritical acceptance of its basic dispositions and tenets. In this final chapter, I want to take an extended look at how the hermeneutic disposition keeps composition theory's description of writing squarely within the representational paradigm. Then I want to argue that hermeneutics has so transformed two of composition studies' core models with which to think about writing—rhetoric and the subject—that we should now set them aside, because the cost to reclaim them would not be repaid.

Moreover, I believe that if we can account for writing without recourse to the subject, we will come closer to describing its proliferation and circulation in an increasingly networked world than we currently are. In *Rescuing the Subject*, Miller wrote that writing is "a process that fictionalizes stability" (*Rescuing* 149). This may have seemed true in 1989, before e-mail and the Internet. But today, when writing pours forth from countless computers and travels to multiple places around the world instantly, simultaneously, and continuously, Miller's postmodern proposition seems less certain. Just as representation does not account for all the functions of writing, today more than ever the fiction of stability does not entirely explain writing's work in the world.

I will first examine composition theory's adherence to the hermeneutic tradition of twentieth-century rhetorical theory, even in attempts to reclaim classical rhetoric for use in current situations. This tradition unnecessarily mystifies and, in effect, romanticizes the subject while presenting an abstruse articulation of the relationship between the supposed "individual" and various aspects of "the world." In turn, this romanticized, hermeneutic subject pervades composition studies, constraining attempts to theorize the reproduction and circulation of writing.

Rhetorical Theory

As one of the earliest and most widely accepted intellectual traditions brought to bear on writing by people in composition studies, rhetorical theory has long enjoyed (and conferred) intellectual status in the field. Even in the work of those who do not explicitly refer to rhetorical theory, some notion of rhetoric often is implied. The fact that some in composition studies consider their work to be more adequately described as "rhetoric" illustrates the rhetorical tradition's power and the field's belief in its ability to grant legitimacy. But even when it has been fused with one or another version of postmodern theory, over the last thirty years rhetorical theory itself has not broken very much new ground, adhering instead to a hermeneutic/epistemic orientation or to debates over that orientation's merits. Attached in this way to hermeneutics, rhetorical theory has been unable to update its traditional notions of agency. In fact, to the extent that rhetoric in the twentieth century has been theorized as a general hermeneutic, it prescribes a highly individualized and prediscursive notion of the subject, one that cannot help composition studies account, theoretically or empirically, for the current production and circulation of writing. Thus, while rhetoric in this sense might lend some institutional legitimacy to composition studies, it does not resolve or address many theoretical issues concerning writing.

But twentieth-century rhetorical theory is only one part of the rhetorical tradition. Classical rhetoric enjoys longer standing as the preferred source of legitimation in composition studies. In addition to now-canonical applications by scholars such as Edward P. J. Corbett and James Kinneavy, theorists such as Sharon Crowley, Susan Jarratt, Kathleen Welch, Victor Vitanza, Jasper Neel, and others have tried to reclaim and readjust some notion of classical rhetoric to match postmodern concerns about agency and discourse in order to arrive at a satisfying account of writing, one that disavows modernist essentialism regarding the status of both the subject and knowledge. In short, these writers have first retheorized rhetoric in order to then discuss writing.

If we set aside questions about the merits of these writers' particular cases, a more fundamental set of problems emerges. First, the theoretical benefit of aligning classical rhetoric with postmodern theory is unclear. If the framework provided by classical rhetoric requires such retrofitting, it is most probably (as some have already argued) inadequate to the task of addressing current conditions of writing.[1] But more importantly, when we update classical rhetoric with postmodern theory, more often than not we to bring it into the broad discourse of late-twentieth-century hermeneutics. So a refurbished classical rhetoric continues to invoke the same subject it had invoked previously. Some *one* must speak, even if the content of that speech is culturally overdetermined. Likewise, in twentieth-century rhetorical/hermeneutic theory, some *one* must interpret, even if that process is culturally overdetermined. Composition theorists might be better off foregoing such theoretical rehabilitation projects and instead approaching writing differently, on different terms. An essentially hermeneutic (or hermeneuticized) theory of rhetoric will only produce, when applied, a hermeneutic theory of writing. And, as I will argue below, a hermeneutic theory of writing is by definition representationalist. Thus, it offers no alternative to theoretical assumptions that have held sway in composition studies for more than a decade.

Some in composition studies will object to setting rhetoric aside in this way. Doing so will seem counterintuitive, given composition studies' long association with rhetoric. But even scholars in rhetoric find rhetoric's entanglement with hermeneutics to be a significant problem, and some of them have tried to free rhetoric from the perceived grip of hermeneutics. For example, in 1997, rhetorical theorist Dilip Parameshwar Gaonkar traced the popularity of hermeneutic rhetoric in the twentieth century to a particular classical tradition. Gaonkar noted that while the "orator perfectus" tradition of Isocrates, Cicero, and Quintilian had long been the dominant mode of Western rhetorical instruction, the twentieth-century revival of rhetoric was mainly Platonic and Aristotelian (27). This accounted for the popularity and influence of hermeneutic theories of rhetoric, of the *rhetorica utens* tradition, which emphasized the act of interpretation, rather than the *rhetorica docens* tradition, which was "a pedagogically motivated network of critical terms, practical devices, prudential rules, and semitheoretical formulations regarding a set of interrelated topics: practical reasoning, figurative language, compositional structures and strategies, psychology of audience, and sociology of opinion" (27). Rather than concerning itself with "the epistemic status of rhetoric," Gaonkar argued, the "orator perfectus" tradition "viewed rhetoric as a civic force rather than a mode of understanding" (27). Any theorizing about rhetoric "was dominated by a pedagogical interest in performance rather than by a 'hermeneutic' interest in understanding" (27). But in the twentieth century, rhetoric was universalized and adapted to the reflective inclinations of its academic proponents, who were "more interested in rhetoric as interpretive theory than as cultural practice" (Gaonkar 27).

Likewise, Victor Vitanza's "Critical Sub/Versions of the History of Philosophical Rhetoric" tried to envision "a Rhetoric that not only *is without* the philosophical pretensions of adjudicating 'philosophical knowledge claims' but also (and more importantly) *is without the philosophical-Rhetorical pretensions of adjudicating 'hermeneutical understandings'*" (42). Vitanza insisted that this "post-philosophical" approach to rhetoric should not be that of "any early or late Neo-Aristotelian, whether it be Richard McKeon or Chaim Perelman or even, at times, Kenneth Burke" (42). Instead, Vitanza called for a metadisciplinary rhetoric that would encompass philosophy and literary theory. Taking a historical cue from the sophistic tradition and a theoretical cue from certain articulations of literary and cultural criticism, he proposed an orientation toward rhetoric that he thought might substantially alter current approaches to writing instruction (43–44). A key component of this proposed reorientation was the rejection of any mediation between rhetoric and philosophy, on the grounds that such attempts inevitably end up privileging philosophy. According to Vitanza, "[E]very attempt to try to reconcile both philosophy and Rhetoric—from Aristotle through Perelman—has been done primarily at the expense of Sophistic Rhetoric and in the name of philosophy itself. . . . Hence, a " 'philosophical rhetoric'" (54). For Vitanza, the revival of rhetoric in the twentieth century had been largely a philosophico-hermeneutic affair. Rhetoric had been theorized narrowly as an instrument of interpretation, and interpretation in turn had been imagined as the paradigmatic human activity. Vitanza was trying to save rhetoric from philosophy and hermeneutics in order to discuss language on different terms.

But whether we try to reclaim a lost tradition of rhetoric or liberate it from the prison-house of philosophy, we are still dealing with a discourse (i.e., a tradition, a body of texts, a collection of theories) that is not equipped even today to address writing beyond the measure of the individual. Gaonkar may or may not be correct, strictly speaking, in his assessment of twentieth-century rhetoric and its relation to that which preceded it. Vitanza may or may not have arrived at a theory of rhetoric from which the shackles of philosophy have been removed. But neither has sufficiently accounted for the potential influence of hermeneutic ideology over nearly every aspect of such contemporary discussions. Each asserts the ability to discuss rhetoric as such, or at least in contexts free from hermeneutic discourse. But I doubt this can happen. I doubt that their reclamations, retrofittings, or retrospectives would not in turn be subsumed by the pervasive hermeneutic paradigm. Gaonkar in particular seems to believe that the word *rhetoric* can represent various *things*, and that the relevant issue is to determine which *thing* ought to be represented by it.

My point is that a great deal of analysis would be needed in order to arrive at a distilled, agreed-upon, and sufficiently precise articulation of "rhetoric," and even then there would be more debate. This would not be bad, in and of itself, except that it would have little to do, theoretically speaking, with writing. Rather, as I mentioned at the beginning of this chapter, it would have to do with the various effects of writing. Of course, the problem of working on the margins of writing rather than on writing itself is what this book has tried to address. We are easily distracted by quasi-theoretical discussions on certain products of writing (such as the "concept" of "rhetoric"), but we tend not to address their function *as* products.

Throughout the 1990s and into this decade, composition theory was more or less blind to this phenomenon. Instead, it took to seeing interpretation, rather than writing, as a paradigmatic feature of human being. The persistent and pervasive assumption that an act of interpretation lies at the heart of discursive activity is considerable and not easily overturned. Certainly, hermeneutics has a rich theoretical history, especially in the twentieth century, as scholars such as Richard Palmer have made clear. Moreover, interpretation is a complex human act worthy of sustained inquiry. But twentieth-century hermeneutic theory— and the rhetorical theory that emerges from it—requires that writing be conceived in the last instance as a vehicle for the delivery of preexisting and non-written content. That is, it requires a representationalist and instrumentalist disposition toward discourse in general and writing in particular—a disposition that, as I argued in chapter 4, composition studies had been empirically and theoretically dismantling until the late 1980s.

It becomes necessary, then, to displace the interpretive stance at the core of composition studies' implicit (and sometimes explicit) dispositions toward writing, which identify it as a technology, as a means of conveying or producing *something else*. This means displacing hermeneutic rhetoric, and perhaps rhetoric altogether. Toward this end, I will examine an explicit argument for a rhetorico-hermeneutic approach to writing, in order to show how its theory of the subject conforms to the traditional, representationalist paradigm and therefore says little that is new about writing. In *Rescuing the Subject*, Miller argued that traditional rhetoric was inadequate to the task of describing and explaining written textuality, so she argued for "textual rhetoric." By extension, I argue that rhetoric may be so overdetermined by the hermeneutic paradigm as to make such a goal not only impossible but also undesirable.

Rhetoric and Hermeneutics in Composition Theory

While hermeneutic rhetoric enjoys hegemony in composition theory and thus operates at the level of assumption, some texts argue for it explicitly. George Pullman's "Rhetoric and Hermeneutics: Composition, Invention, and Literature" is one such example, and as such it provides many occasions to examine not only the assumptions of hermeneutic rhetoric but also its consequences for a theory of writing. Pullman draws on Gadamer's hermeneutic theory to arrive at a theory of writing that places the act of interpretation at the necessary beginning of any discursive activity. In doing so, his argument endorses a more complex version of the old Platonic/Cartesian subject. Ironically, then, the very essentialism that Pullman seeks to undo via reference to hermeneutic theory is actually a key component of that theory.

By considering interpretation to be "a specialized application of topical invention," Pullman proposes to formally integrate hermeneutics and rhetoric (368). In this formulation, invention is "a creative effort to compose an understanding" (369). A crucial concept in philosophical hermeneutics, "understanding," according to Pullman, makes rhetoric an "epistemic activity" and not just the arrangement of preexisting information (369). If invention is the heart of rhetoric, and interpretation is a special topic of invention, then rhetoric is fundamentally hermeneutic. Furthermore, according to this argument, and following Gadamer directly, hermeneutics is itself fundamentally rhetorical. According to Pullman, this "rhetorization of hermeneutics," whereby hermeneutics is articulated as "a performance-centered form of argumentation" as well as "an unavoidable activity of life in general," erases the distinction between the formerly abstract processes of learning/understanding and the formerly technical processes of inventing/writing (376–378). In this scheme, "the purpose of writing is not to represent thought in words or to convey abstract meanings to others by means of words, but rather to exert power over experience—to reform what had been formed before" (379).

Critiques of philosophical hermeneutics are well established and need not be rehearsed in detail. It is enough here to point out its essentialism, whereby it reserves systemic and uncritical conceptual space for *something* nondiscursive. In the lexicon of philosophical hermeneutics, and in Pullman's argument, the term *experience* occupies such a space. It signifies existential immediacy, that which is lived first and articulated later, when it is reformed in the act of writing. In other words, *experience* happens first, then it comes into language, is written down. Gadamer himself notes as much when, despite having insisted that experience "is not wordless to begin with," he nonetheless explains that "experience of itself seeks and finds words that express it" (*Truth* 417). Gadamer ascribes agency to the concept of experience; that is, experience *seeks* and *finds* host words. This is a familiar strategy of philosophical hermeneutics, one that invokes a noumenal realm to which interpretation is ultimately addressed, a realm accessed via the secondary *event* of language. Following Gadamer's view on language, Pullman distinguishes between a generative, speculative function of writing and the mere representation of thoughts or the conveying of abstractions through writing by offering a more constructive, participatory version of writing. For Pullman, the salient feature of writing is its ability to create, rather than merely transmit, a meaning.

This distinction between writing-as-generation and writing-as-representation is not entirely new to composition studies, though its justification through hermeneutic theory is innovative. Researchers and teachers in the field have long held that writing is complex activity involving a good deal more than the straightforward representation of ideas through words. In fact, few today would argue with that assertion. Thus, hermeneutic rhetoric seems very well suited to composition studies insofar as both appear to appreciate the richness of writing. Further, it seems appropriate to differentiate between generative and representative functions of writing—and to value the former over the latter—because to say that people can generate meaning (however overdetermined) with writing is to say that they have access to something not simply contained in words but somehow evoked or even conjured with them. This idea is much more appealing than that of mere representation, where work with words appears to be no more conceptually intricate than the packing and unpacking of suitcases, requiring no academic discipline devoted to its study.

But both writing-as-generation and writing-as-representation adhere to the concept of *meaning*, thus they are equally essentialist. Proponents of writing-as-generation will claim that the difference between the two is consequential, and to an extent they are probably correct. I am simply claiming that their similarities are more consequential.

Whether we claim that writing makes or transmits, in both cases we affirm the presence of something that is not writing itself, and we give it the title of *meaning*. At other times, we might name it with more specificity, perhaps calling it an *idea*, a *concept*, an *experience*, the *tradition*, and so on. But none of these are the same as writing. They are the stuff, the content, the *things* that writing must represent, because it is not any of them itself. In this sense, writing-as-generation is a more complex version of writing-as-representation, one that differs primarily on the question of origins. Hermeneutic rhetoric, then, complicates the processes of representation, but it operates squarely within the traditional paradigm of representation.

Writing Without Subjects

If a hermeneutically oriented theory of writing is not substantially different from a representationalist theory, then it cannot help us describe writing differently. What remains, then, is to explain that the cultural work that *is* writing is more complex, more pervasive, and therefore more worthy of sustained intellectual inquiry than the content conveyed *in* writing by individual subjects. The category of the subject, regardless of how it is articulated, invokes an individual consciousness interacting with a fundamentally separate world, much as hermeneutics does. But as theorists such as Karen Burke Lefevre and, more recently, Arabella Lyon have pointed out, individual volition makes little theoretical or empirical sense when we consider the interconnectedness and fluidity that increasingly characterizes contemporary scenes of writing.

As composition theorists, if we work in the realm of agents, subjects, or consciousness, then our descriptions of writing will only ever present it as an instrument, as a means by which *something else* is arrived at. But if we give up the deep-seated and ultimately unfounded assumption that writing is a function and product of individuals interacting with the world, with culture, with tradition, or even with themselves, then we might begin to address the many implications of the proposition that writing is a phenomenon of constant (re)circulation, one that promises the representation of *something else* but never actually delivers. There is no theory of the subject that can contribute to this.

This claim echoes some of the standard claims of post-structuralist theory, and so some in composition studies might argue that it is too abstract to be of use. But the prospect of such familiar resistance suggests that the terms on which the field discusses writing are themselves overdetermined, bound by theory and practice at either end of a continuum. According to these terms, writing is either of obscure design, purpose, and origin, or it is a mere tool by which to get things done. Sometimes both conceptions can be valued simultaneously or in some kind of relation. But in the end, these options, together or apart, do not adequately describe what writing is and how it works.

Also, it might be argued that composition theory has already taken into account the profoundly social nature of language, that it has already recognized the need to situate the writing subject and the act of writing within complex networks of cultural, political, ideological, and hegemonic forces. But the main result of the social turn in composition theory has been the installation of a traditional, even Romantic, writing subject into those complex networks—in effect, a version of hermeneutic theory's achievement. The writing subject itself, as I have been arguing variously throughout this book, has remained relatively untouched, untheorized. And the result has been the persistence of a theoretical disposition that continues to understand the act of writing as an individual's rendering of experience in graphic form. Consequently, it seems nearly impossible and largely impractical to continue working with the category of "subject" because, like "rhetoric," the work of reclaiming it would be fraught with peril and, in the end, quite possibly beside the point. It is perhaps not an overstatement to say that more progress was made toward theorizing writing in the 1970s and early 1980s than has been made in the last twenty years, despite the emergence of "the subject" as a category of discussion.

So writing exceeds the idea of representation, as well as the idea of the subject. As the previous chapters have already shown, Derrida's writings from the late 1960s and early 1970s make this case. Unfortunately, as Gregory Ulmer has noted, studies of those works—and of Derrida's corpus in general—tend to emphasize the analytic that is deconstruction rather than the methodology that is grammatology. That is, Derrida's work is generally understood as a guide to the reception of written discourse (i.e., as a hermeneutic) rather than as a prompt for new models of the reproduction and circulation of written discourse (i.e., as a heuristic, or to use Ulmer's term, a "heuretic"). For composition studies—and for composition theory in particular—this distinction between deconstruction and grammatology is crucial because it helps confront the theoretical problems that I have been detailing in this book: problems having to do with mistaking such strategic terms as knowledge, ideology, and rhetoric for general concepts. More to the point, the emphasis on grammatology over deconstruction, on heuristic/heuretic over hermeneutic, allows one to place in doubt the very notion of a general concept. When, in the study of writing, basic questions focus not on meanings conveyed *in* or *through* or *by* acts of writing (the representational/instrumentalist paradigm) but on connections (re)made *among* and *across* endlessly generated (f)acts of writing, then the idea that there is *something else* apart from writing, driving writing, becomes suspect. In fact, it becomes possible to consider that the very notion of *something else*, regardless of how it manifests in particular instances, is itself a function of writing. The idea of *something else*, the idea of meaning, even the idea of "the idea," turn out to be structural functions of the (f)act of writing rather than metaphysical, philosophical, or even merely theoretical concepts.

Under this paradigm, the job of the composition theorist changes. Composition theory since the late 1980s had set out to broaden the field's scope of inquiry *beyond* writing, toward perceived forces that in various ways made their presence felt *through* the instrument or medium of writing. Furthermore, composition theory had also determined that writing itself could be construed more broadly as discourse, language, or rhetoric, thus offering even more ways to expand the range of issues the field could raise. But these strategies only work to the extent that writing itself could be taken for granted. Now, composition theory can remind the rest of the field that writing is not only at the center of composition studies, but that it is also at the center of all of the various "issues" the field finds important enough to study. Those issues, which had been thought to manifest in discourse, are now more properly understood as effects of writing. Thus, for example, it will make little sense to continue framing the question of the relationship between writing and ideology in terms of the latter's effect on the former. Rather, ideology should be understood as a tactical feature of writing insofar as the term itself marks a particular version of the possibility of *something else*, where *something else* is a structural function of the (f)act of writing, the necessary Other of writing, the promise of communication, without which there is no writing.

In this way, everything, every possible and conceivable "issue," becomes a function of writing. This is certainly a sweeping statement, so sweeping as to be useless if it did not lead directly back to the question of individual bodies. It is one thing to conceptually reorganize the world by giving writing pride of place, as I have done. It is another thing to describe the nature and function of writing bodies in this new paradigm. This is because all of our available terms—agency, subject, consciousness—are so deeply implicated in the representationalist paradigm that it is all but impossible to imagine a writer or even an appropriately postmodernized "writing subject" that is not fundamentally prediscursive, that solves or identifies problems through the medium or tools of language and writing. So a crucial question for composition theory under a new paradigm might be the following: At the level of the individual body, how does the socially and culturally embedded (f)act of writing occur and what can be said about it? This question certainly has been asked in composition studies, most recently by proponents of activity theory. But the question consistently has been asked in the context of the representationalist paradigm, where writing is understood as a tool, however complex, and where cognition, however distributed, stands as the signature gesture of prediscursive consciousness. So the answers have been unsatisfactory.

Likewise, attempts to retheorize invention (as well as other aspects of rhetoric) have fallen short of describing the writing body because of the relation they draw between invention and writing. That is, invention has been assumed to be a part of, yet also apart from, writing. It has not been recognized as yet another of the endless procession of placemarkers for the idea of *something else*. When rhetoric and its canons are taken to represent *something else* directly, rather than to mark the discursively necessary "*something else*" slot, as it were—that is, when *something else* is naturalized—then we remain within the paradigm of representation and the writing body is locked into the role of symbol manipulator, problem solver, consciousness bearer, however attenuated by a host of social and/or cultural factors.

Certainly, this paradigm is and has been very generative. A framework that imagines the circulation of writing to originate in or to pass through, however temporarily, something called "the subject" makes possible a wide range of theoretical and empirical work. If we can take for granted the very notion of the subject, regardless of how it is specifically theorized, then we can do two things. First, we can assume that writing is "meaningful" activity, made so by its relation to the subject, which is a generating and/or transforming entity: generating when it is imagined to initiate the flow of writing, transforming when it alters or rearranges particular elements in the flow of writing. Second, we can use our empirical and theoretical equipment to make both general and specific statements about patterns of meaning (and meaning making) as well as the nature of meaningfulness itself. These two gestures comprise the history of composition research and theory.

But how might writing be described so as not to take the subject as an unproblematic point of departure? Or, how might writing be theorized and studied in ways that neither assume nor try to account for the problem of agency, that instead see agency as yet another effect of writing? First, I should note that to recognize "the problem of agency" as a problem adhering to the representationalist paradigm of writing is not to make the poststructuralist mistake of trying to retheorize or otherwise account for agency in the face of overwhelming discursiveness. I do not want to reclaim agency. Agency is not a concept that manifests differently at different times, that can be updated as circumstances require, and that must be addressed by any broad theoretical discussion of writing. That is, agency is not a problem to be addressed by a theory of writing. To see it this way is to confer a certain nondiscursive status on "agency" and to confirm a certain relationship between it and writing. And, of course, it is with this and other relationships between "concepts" and writing that this book has been concerned.

To study writing without resorting to agency, without recourse to the subject, is already to approach writing as circulation and reproduction extending, like turtles carrying Earth, "all the way down." It is to scrupulously attend to the mechanisms of reproduction and circulation, whereby writing appears to offer up ideas, concepts, problems, even theories in order to continue the process of reproduction and circulation. For example, it is to recognize that the difference between the traditional term *author* and Foucault's term *author-function* is overstated by postmodernism because both point to an other of writing: the former by asserting a source of writing, the latter by establishing a transfer station for writing in which are produced consequential changes. That is, whether we say that language comes from or passes through the figure of the author, we assert that something of consequence happens to language at that point. It emerges from the author, or the author function, changed. For composition studies, this imagined point or moment of birth or transformation, has been the absolute focus of theory, research, and pedagogy. In this book, I have been arguing that it need not be, that there are other ways to theorize and study writing that do not make a fetish of either the subject or the subject's status as what Kenneth Burke calls the symbol-using animal. I have been arguing that to do so is precisely to focus on representation at the expense of other functions of writing, functions that have little directly to do with the particular activities of particular subjects and their "use" of written language.

What I have been describing, then, is less a theory than a grammar of writing. And, consequently, it may be one of this project's unresolved contradictions that the "writtenness" with which I have tried to burden certain of composition theory's cherished concepts, I do not in turn place upon writing. There is no satisfactory answer to this question, if satisfaction in this case is the resolution of a potential contradiction. Perhaps the best one can do is to confer upon it the status of a paradox. At any rate, we know that perspectives have limitations—that, as Burke notes, "[a] way of seeing is also a way of not seeing" (*Permanence* 49).

Notes

Chapter One. The Current State of Composition Theory

1. See Miller, *Assuming the Positions*.
2. See *Writing and Difference, Of Grammatology, Margins of Philosophy,* and *Dissemination*.
3. See Dasenbrock, Herzberg, Juncker, Smit's "Rhetorical Method," and de Beaugrande.
4. See, for example, Barton and Charney.

Chapter Two. The Discourse of Knowledge in Composition Theory

1. Rorty cites what he calls "Locke's confusion" as another crucial step in the emergence of philosophy-as-epistemology. While Descartes had devised the notion of *mind* that would serve as epistemology's field of study, Locke tried to mark the operational boundaries of that mind. According to Rorty, Locke saw a relation between "a mechanistic account of the operations of our mind and the 'grounding' of our claims to knowledge" (140). That is, he confused an explanation for the development of a belief with the justification of that belief, as if an understanding of how things work also offered an explanation of why they did so. This occurred, according to Rorty, because Locke saw knowledge "as a relation between persons and objects rather than persons and propositions" (142). In such a scenario, propositions—the statements we make about the relation between persons and objects—are representative rather than constitutive, and the work of epistemology is to get at the "essence" of

that relation through the necessary and hopefully transparent medium of language.

Rorty sees Locke not only confusing two separate issues, but doing so for no apparent reason. That is, it is not clear why in the first place one would be led to confuse the formulation of a belief with its justification. But, according to Rorty, this inexplicable situation points to the very problem of epistemology: it seeks rational answers to quasi-theological questions.

2. In addition to Scott's "On Viewing Rhetoric as Epistemic," see the following, among others: Carleton, "What is Rhetorical Knowledge?"; Cherwitz, "Rhetoric as 'A Way of Knowing' "; Cherwitz and Hikins, "Rhetorical Perspectivism" and "Toward a Rhetorical Epistemology"; Farrell, "Knowledge, Consensus, and Rhetorical Theory"; Gregg, "Rhetoric and Knowing"; Leff, "In Search of Ariadne's Thread"; Scott, "On Viewing Rhetoric as Epistemic: Ten Years Later," "On *Not* Defining 'Rhetoric,' " "Non-Discipline as a Remedy for Rhetoric?" and "Rhetoric is Epistemic: What Difference Does that Make?"

In addition, see the "Forum" section of Vol. 76 (1990) of the *Quarterly Journal of Speech*, subtitled "The Reported Demise of Epistemic Rhetoric", which contains contributions from Barry Brummett, Cherwitz and Hikins, and Farrell. See also the Vol. 80 (1994) "Forum," subtitled "Reflections on a Nietzschean Turn in Rhetorical Theory: Rhetoric Without Epistemology?" in which Douglas Thomas responds to a previously published article by Whitson and Poulakos titled "Nietzsche and the Aesthetics of Rhetoric," which I in turn discuss below.

3. See Berlin's overview of epistemic rhetoric in *Rhetoric and Reality*.

4. Also implicit in both composition's and communication studies' discussions of epistemic rhetoric are assumptions about knowledge that, if examined, should lead compositionists to question the need for assenting or adhering to an epistemic rhetoric at all. The ongoing discussions in philosophy that examine the nature, conditions, and limits of knowledge have been taken into account by few in either field. Even a glance at recent work in this area of philosophy indicates that inquiry into the nature and origins of knowledge is a complex endeavor. For one thing, few explicitly identify knowledge with Cartesian certainty anymore, and the traditional definition of *knowledge* as justified true belief has been complicated, extended, and even refuted. In light of this complexity, it should become evident that reducing the question of knowledge to neat and unexamined formulations does little

to further any theoretical explanations of rhetoric or writing. Further-more, Richard Rorty's provocative argument that philosophy's epistemological imperative is historically specific rather than intellectually perennial, and that such an imperative depends on the assertion of a clear distinction between the interior space of the mind and the exterior space of the world, should suggest to compositionists that the entire epistemic enterprise, complex and varied as it is, rests on assumptions that, as rhetoricians, they might find unwarranted.

5. In addition to Neel's crucial book, see Crowley's *A Teacher's Introduction to Deconstruction* and Atkins and Michael L. Johnson's *Writing and Reading Differently*. On a smaller scale, a few others in the field have tackled the subject. Gary Olson's *JAC* interview of Derrida covers a range of issues, including writing, but not in detail. Reed Way Dasenbrock's "Becoming Aware of the Myth of Presence" and Robert Brooke's "Control in Writing" apply certain aspects of Derrida's general theory to issues in composition. Finally, Lester Faigley's *Fragments of Rationality* and John Schilb's *Between the Lines* mention Derrida and his work in the broader contexts of postmodernism and poststructuralism. But the works I've mentioned constitute the range and degree to which Derrida's theoretical statements about writing have been placed in dialogue with composition's own theoretical concerns. Neel suggests that this is the case because Derrida's "analytical methods make every-thing harder, not easier," which conflicts with what Neel sees as our field's "long tradition of seeking the easier, quicker way" (101).

Neel's comment was probably more accurate in 1988 than it is now, when postmodernism of one kind or another (or at least the espousal of it) has become commonplace in composition theory. But even today Neel's claim is not entirely off base. Derrida's work remains among the most challenging and difficult "postmodern" theory to address, and composition's approach to dealing with such difficult work remains to simplify or distill. We perform what amount to passing glances at such work, at times on the way to some pedagogical application perceived as a "payoff" for having read the theory. At other times, we rely on secondhand accounts of primary theoretical texts, thus avoiding the difficult work of critical evaluation so that we can get to the application. This tendency is especially troubling when the theoretical texts in question deal with writing, as do many of Derrida's early works. But we ought not to rely solely on others' synopses, not even on Neel's and Crowley's deft expositions and analyses, to give us

Derrida's theory of writing. Their purpose is not to distill, but to engage us in conversation about potentially useful theoretical work that bears upon our objects of study—theoretical work that we other theorists ought to read, study, and write about with the same care that they do, because to do so is in our disciplinary and intellectual interests.

Chapter Three. Composition's Ideology Apparatus

1. For example, see France, Mutnick, and Sidler & Morris.

2. This statement is part of her critique of Foucault. According to Spivak, his work's inability to attend to "the subject-constituting register of ideology because of its tenacious commitment to the sub-individual and, at the other end, the great aggregative apparatuses" forces Foucault to assume "'the empirical subject, the intending subject, the self even." (252).

3. In addition to Alcorn and Murphy as early engagements with, rather than applications of, Berlin's work, see Harkin. Also, see Ballif, McComiskey, and Paine as more recent responses to Berlin's call. Ballif, in particular, is interested in the theoretical dimensions of Berlin's work rather than its pedagogical ramifications.

4. In fact, the language of "equivalences" and "levels" anticipates Laclau and Mouffe's critical lexicon in *Hegemony and Socialist Strategy.*

5. *Bootstraps* subordinates rhetoric to hegemony, however, in the same way that Berlin's work subordinates rhetoric to ideology. Villaneuva writes: "Rhetoric, after all, is how ideologies are carried, how hegemonies are maintained. Rhetoric, then, would be the means by which hegemonies could be countered" (121).

Chapter Four. Theories of Culture in Composition Theory

1. See Arabella Lyon's *Intentions: Negotiated, Contested, and Ignored* for a critique of Mailloux's rhetorical hermeneutics and of rhetorical hermeneutics in general.

2. A more thorough intellectual history of the field than that which I offer here can be found in Nystrand et al., "Where Did Composition Studies Come From?"

3. Nystrand et al., identify an even earlier parallel between composition and literary theory. They connect Stanley Fish's early work in reader-response criticism to Emig's study of composing processes, arguing that both "sought to focus scholarly attention away from the text and onto the cognitive processes of the writer/reader, characterizing these processes in dynamic, temporal terms" (282). Furthermore, they argue, both are informed by "constructivist premises about knowing, meaning, and language processes" that were drawn from linguistics (283).

4. This essay was originally published in Greenblatt and Gunn's edited collection, *Redrawing the Boundaries*, but I will be citing the version published in Bhabha's *The Location of Culture*.

Chapter Five. Writing Without Subjects

1. Of course, as far back as 1982 Knoblauch and Brannon had argued against the classical tradition's usefulness for contemporary composition studies, claiming that "modern" and more accurate notions of discourse were better suited to the task of informing composition pedagogy. But according to my argument, the "modern" dispositions they advocate merely recast the basic problem of the subject, rather than resolve it.

Works Cited

Alcorn, Marshall W., Jr. "Changing the Subject of Postmodernist Theory: Discourse, Ideology, and Therapy in the Classroom." *Rhetoric Review* 13 (1995): 331–49.

Althusser, Louis. *"Lenin and Philosophy" and Other Essays*. Trans. Ben Brewster. New York: Monthly Review P, 1971.

———. "Lenin Before Hegel." *"Lenin and Philosophy" and Other Essays*. 107–25.

———. "Ideology and Ideological State Apparatuses (Notes Toward an Investigation)." *"Lenin and Philosophy" and Other Essays*. 127–86.

———. *For Marx*. Trans. Ben Brewster. New York: Verso, 1996 (1969).

Atkins, G. Douglas, and Michael L. Johnson, eds. *Writing and Reading Differently: Deconstruction and the Teaching of Composition and Literature*. Lawrence, KS: University Press of Kansas, 1985.

Ballif, Michelle. *Seduction, Sophistry, and the Woman with the Rhetorical Figure*. Carbondale: Southern Illinois UP, 2001.

Bartholomae, David. "Inventing the University." *Composition in Four Keys*.

Bartholomae, David, and Anthony R. Petrosky, eds. *Facts, Artifacts, and Counterfacts: Theory and Method for a Reading and Writing Course*. Portsmouth, NH: Boynton/Cook, 1986.

Barton, Ellen. "Empirical Studies in Composition." *College English* 59 (1997): 815–27.

Baudrillard, Jean. *The Perfect Crime*. Trans. Chris Turner. New York: Verso, 1996.

———. *Simulacra and Simulation*. Trans. Sheila Faria Glaser. Ann Arbor: U of Michigan P, 1994.

Berkenkotter, Carol. "The Legacy of Positivism in Empirical Composition Research." *Journal of Advanced Composition* 9 (1989): 69–82.

Berkenkotter, Carol, and Thomas N. Huckin. *Genre Knowledge in Disciplinary Communication: Cognition/Culture/Power.* Northvale, NJ: Erlbaum, 1995.

Berlin, James A. "Poststructuralism, Semiotics, and Social-Epistemic Rhetoric: Converging Agendas." Enos and Brown 137–53.

———. "Rhetoric and Ideology in the Writing Class." *College English* 50 (1988): 477–94.

———. *Rhetoric and Reality: Writing Instruction in American Colleges, 1900–1985.* Carbondale: Southern Illinois UP, 1987.

———. *Rhetorics, Poetics, and Cultures: Refiguring College English Studies.* Urbana: NCTE, 1996.

Berlin, James A., and Michael J. Vivion. *Cultural Studies in the English Classroom.* Portsmouth, NH: Boynton/Cook, 1992.

Berthoff, Ann E. *The Making of Meaning: Metaphors, Models, and Maxims for Teachers.* Portsmouth, NH: Boynton/Cook, 1981.

Bhabha, Homi K. "The Postcolonial and the Postmodern: The Question of Agency." *The Location of Culture.* New York: Routledge, 1994. 171–97.

Bizzell, Patricia. *Academic Discourse and Critical Consciousness.* Pittsburgh: U of Pittsburgh P, 1992.

Brooke, Robert. "Control in Writing: Flower, Derrida, and Images of the Writer." *College English* 51 (1989): 405–17.

Bruffee, Kenneth. "Collaborative Learning and the 'Conversation of Mankind.' " *College English* 46 (1984): 635–52.

Burke, Kenneth. *Counter-Statement.* Berkeley: U of California P, 1968 (1931).

———. *A Rhetoric of Motives.* Berkeley: U of California P, 1969 (1950).

Butler, Judith. *The Psychic Life of Power: Theories in Subjection.* Stanford: Stanford UP, 1997.

Bygrave, Stephen. *Kenneth Burke: Rhetoric and Ideology.* New York: Routledge, 1993.

Carleton, Walter M. "What is Rhetorical Knowledge? A Response to Farrell—And More." *Quarterly Journal of Speech* 64 (1978): 313–28.

Center for Contemporary Cultural Studies. *On Ideology.* London: Hutchinson, 1978.

Charney, Davida. "Empiricism is not a Four-Letter Word." *College Composition and Communication* 47 (1996): 567–93.

Cherwitz, Richard. "Rhetoric as a 'Way of Knowing': An Attenuation of the Epistemological Claims of the 'New Rhetoric.' " *Southern Speech Communication Journal* 42 (1977): 207–19.

Cherwitz, Richard A., and James W. Hikins. "Rhetorical Perspectivism." *Quarterly Journal of Speech* 69 (1983): 249–66.

———. "Toward a Rhetorical Epistemology." *Southern Speech Communication Journal* 47 (1982): 135–62.

Chow, Rey. *Writing Diaspora: Tactics of Intervention in Contemporary Cultural Studies.* Bloomington: Indiana UP, 1993.

Cooper, Charles R., and Susan Peck MacDonald. *Writing the World: Reading and Writing about Issues of the Day.* New York: Bedford/St. Martin's, 1999.

Crowley, Sharon. *A Teacher's Introduction to Deconstruction.* Urbana: NCTE, 1990.

Culler, Jonathan. *On Deconstruction: Theory and Criticism after Structuralism.* Ithaca: Cornell UP, 1982.

Dasenbrock, Reed Way. "Becoming Aware of the Myth of Presence." Olson and Dobrin 82–92.

Davis, D. Diane. *Breaking Up [at] Totality: A Rhetoric of Laughter.* Carbondale: Southern Illinois UP, 2000.

De Beaugrande, Robert. "In Search of Feminist Discourse: The 'Difficult' Case of Luce Irigaray." *College English* 50 (1988): 253–72.

Derrida, Jacques. *Dissemination.* Trans. Barbara Johnson. Chicago: U of Chicago P, 1981.

———. *Of Grammatology,* corrected ed. Trans. Gayatri Chakravorty Spivak. Baltimore: Johns Hopkins UP, 1997.

———. "Signature Event Context." *Margins of Philosophy.* Trans. Alan Bass. Chicago: U of Chicago P, 1982. 307–30.

————. *Writing and Difference.* Trans. Alan Bass. Chicago, U of Chicago P, 1978.

Dobrin, Sidney I. *Constructing Knowledges: The Politics of Theory-Building and Pedagogy in Composition.* Albany: State U of New York P, 1997.

Elbow, Peter. *Writing Without Teachers.* New York: Oxford UP, 1973.

Emig, Janet. *The Composing Processes of Twelfth Graders.* Urbana: NCTE, 1971.

————. "Writing as a Mode of Learning." *Cross-Talk in Comp Theory: A Reader.* Ed. Victor Villanueva Jr. Urbana: NCTE, 1997. 7–15.

Enos, Theresa, and Stuart C. Brown, eds. *Defining the New Rhetorics.* Newbury Park, CA: Sage, 1993.

Ervin, Elizabeth. "Epistemology." *Keywords in Composition Studies.* Ed. Paul Heilker and Peter Vandenberg. Portsmouth, NH: Boynton/Cook, 1996. 76–80.

Faigley, Lester. *Fragments of Rationality: Postmodernity and the Subject of Composition.* Pittsburgh: U of Pittsburgh P, 1992.

Farrell, Thomas B. "Knowledge, Consensus, and Rhetorical Theory." *Quarterly Journal of Speech* 62 (1976): 1–14.

Fish, Stanley. "Consequences." *Doing What Comes Naturally: Change, Rhetoric, and the Practice of Theory in Literary and Legal Studies.* Durham: Duke UP, 1990. 315–41.

Flower, Linda. "Observation-Based Theory Building." Olson, *Rhetoric* 163–85.

"The Forum: Reflections on a Nietzschean Turn in Rhetorical Theory: Rhetoric Without Epistemology?" *Quarterly Journal of Speech* 80 (1994): 71–76.

"The Forum: The Reported Demise of Epistemic Rhetoric." *Quarterly Journal of Speech* 76 (1990): 69–84.

Foucault, Michel. "What is an Author?" The Foucault Reader. Ed. Paul Rabinow. New York: Pantheon, 1984. 101–20.

————. *The Order of Things: An Archaeology of the Human Sciences.* New York: Vintage, 1973 (1970).

France, Alan W. *Composition as a Cultural Practice.* Westport, CT: Bergin and Garvey, 1994.

Gaonkar, Dilip Parameshwar. "The Idea of Rhetoric in the Rhetoric of Science." *Rhetorical Hermeneutics: Invention and Interpretation in the Age of Science.* Ed. Alan G. Gross and William M. Keith. Albany: State U of New York P, 1997.

Grassi, Ernesto. *Rhetoric as Philosophy: The Humanist Tradition.* University Park: Penn State UP, 1980.

Greenblatt, Stephen, and Giles Gunn. *Redrawing the Boundaries: The Transformation of English and American Literary Studies.* New York: MLA, 1992.

Gregg, Richard B. "Rhetoric and Knowing: The Search for Perspective." *Central States Speech Journal* 32 (1981): 133–44.

Guillory, John. *Cultural Capital: The Problem of Literary Canon Formation.* Chicago: U of Chicago P, 1993.

Hairston, Maxine. "The Winds of Change: Thomas Kuhn and the Revolution in the Teaching of Writing." *College Composition and Communication* 33 (1982): 76–88.

Harkin, Patricia. "In the Crossfire: (after) Jim Berlin." *Works and Days* 14 (1996): 291–98.

Harkin, Patricia, and John Schilb. *Contending With Words: Composition and Rhetoric in a Postmodern Age.* New York: MLA, 1991.

Herzberg, Bruce. "Michel Foucault's Rhetorical Theory." Harkin and Schilb 69–81.

Judovitz, Dalia. *Subjectivity and Representation in Descartes: The Origins of Modernity.* Cambridge: Cambridge UP, 1988.

Juncker, Clara. "Writing (with) Cixous." *College English* 50 (1988): 424–36.

Kent, Thomas. "The Consequences of Theory for the Practice of Writing." Olson and Taylor 147–61.

———. "Paralogic Rhetoric: An Overview." Olson, *Rhetoric*, 143–52.

Knapp, Steven, and Walter Benn Michaels. "Against Theory." *Against Theory: Literary Studies and the New Pragmatism.* Ed. W. J. T. Mitchell. Chicago: U of Chicago P, 1985. 11–30.

Laclau, Ernesto, and Chantal Mouffe. *Hegemony and Socialist Strategy.* New York: Verso, 1985.

Lauer, Janice M. "Composition Studies: Dappled Discipline." *Rhetoric Review* 3 (1984): 20–29.

Leff, Michael C. "In Search of Ariadne's Thread: A Review of the Recent Literature on Rhetorical Theory." *Central States Speech Journal* 29 (1978): 73–91.

Lentricchia, Frank. *Criticism and Social Change.* Chicago: U of Chicago P, 1985.

Lu, Min-Zhan. "Conflict and Struggle: The Enemies or Preconditions of Basic Writing?" *College English* 54 (1992): 887–913.

Lyon, Arabella. *Intentions: Negotiated, Contested, and Ignored.* University Park: Penn State UP, 1998.

Macrorie, Ken. *Uptaught.* Portsmouth, NH: Boynton/Cook, 1996 (1970).

Mailloux, Steven. *Rhetorical Power.* Ithaca: Cornell UP, 1989.

McComiskey, Bruce. *Teaching Composition as a Social Process.* Logan: Utah State UP, 2000.

McQuade, Donald, and Christine McQuade. *Seeing and Writing 2.* New York: Bedford/St. Martin's, 2003.

Miller, Susan. *Assuming the Positions: Cultural Pedagogy and the Practice of Commonplace Writing.* Pittsburgh: U of Pittsburgh P, 1999.

———. "Composition as a Cultural Artifact: Rethinking History as Theory." *Writing Theory and Critical Theory.* Ed. John Clifford and John Schilb. New York: MLA, 1994. 19–32.

———. *Rescuing the Subject: A Critical Introduction to Rhetoric and the Writer.* Carbondale: Southern Illinois UP, 1989.

———. "Technologies of Self(?)-Formation." *JAC* 17 (1997): 497–500.

Murphy, Michael. "After Progressivism: Modern Composition, Institutional Service, and Cultural Studies." *Composition Theory for the Postmodern Classroom.* Ed. Gary A. Olson and Sidney I. Dobrin. Albany: State U of New York P, 1994. 205–24.

Mutnick, Deborah. *Writing in an Alien World: Basic Writing and the Struggle for Equality in Higher Education.* Portsmouth, NH: Boynton/Cook, 1996.

Neel, Jasper. *Plato, Derrida, and Writing.* Carbondale: Southern Illinois UP, 1988.

Newkirk, Thomas. *The Performance of Self in Student Writing*. Portsmouth, NH: Boynton/Cook, 1997.

Nystrand, Martin, Stuart Greene, and Jeffrey Wiemelt. "Where Did Composition Studies Come From? An Intellectual History." *Written Communication* 10 (1993): 267–333.

Olson, Gary A. "Jane Tompkins and the Politics of Writing, Scholarship, and Pedagogy." *JAC* 15 (1995): 1–17.

———. "The Death of Composition as an Intellectual Discipline." *Rhetoric and Composition as Intellectual Work*. Ed. Gary Olson. Carbondale: Southern Illinois UP, 2002.

Olson, Gary A., and Sidney I. Dobrin, eds. *Composition Theory for the Postmodern Classroom*. Albany: State U of New York P, 1994.

Olson, Gary A., and Todd W. Taylor, eds. *Publishing in Rhetoric and Composition*. Albany: State U of New York P, 1997.

Paine, Charles. *The Resistant Writer: Rhetoric as Immunity, 1850 to the Present*. Albany: State U of New York P, 1999.

Petraglia, Joseph. "Interrupting the Conversation: The Constructionist Dialogue in Composition." Olson and Dobrin 313–31.

Pullman, George. "Rhetoric and Hermeneutics: Composition, Invention, and Literature." *JAC* 14 (1994): 367–87.

Rickert, Thomas J. "Engaging Modernisms, Emerging Posthumanisms, and the Rhetorics of Doing." *JAC* 20 (2000): 672–84.

Ricoeur, Paul. *Freud and Philosophy: An Essay on Interpretation*. Trans. Denis Savage. New Haven: Yale UP, 1970.

Robison, Lori. "'This Could Have Been Me': Composition and the Implications of Cultural Perspective." Berlin and Vivion 231–43.

Rorty, Richard. *Philosophy and the Mirror of Nature*. Princeton: Princeton UP, 1979.

Royer, Daniel J. "New Challenges to Epistemic Rhetoric." *Rhetoric Review* 9 (1991): 282–97.

Said, Edward W. *Orientalism*. New York: Vintage, 1979.

Salvatori, Mariolina. "The Dialogical Nature of Basic Reading and Writing." Bartholomae and Petrosky 137–66.

Schilb, John. *Between the Lines: Relating Composition Theory and Literary Theory.* Portsmouth, NH: Boynton/Cook, 1996.

Schriner, Delores K. "One Person, Many Worlds: A Multi-Cultural Composition Curriculum." Berlin and Vivion 95–111.

Scott, Robert L. "Non-Discipline as a Remedy for Rhetoric? A Reply to Victor Vitanza." *Rhetoric Review* 6 (1988): 233–37.

———. "On *Not* Defining Rhetoric." *Philosophy and Rhetoric* 6 (1973): 81–96.

———. "On Viewing Rhetoric as Epistemic." *Central States Speech Journal* 18 (1967): 9–17.

———. "Rhetoric is Epistemic: What Difference Does That Make?" Enos and Brown. 120–36.

Shaughnessy, Mina P. *Errors and Expectations: A Guide for the Teacher of Basic Writing.* New York: Oxford UP, 1977.

Sidler, Michelle, and Richard Morris. "Writing in a Post-Berlinian Landscape: Cultural Composition in the Classroom." *JAC* 18 (1998): 275–91.

Smit, David W. "Hall of Mirrors: Antifoundationalist Theory and the Teaching of Writing." *JAC* 15 (1995): 35–52.

———. "The Rhetorical Method of Ludwig Wittgenstein." *Rhetoric Review* 10 (1991): 31–51.

Spivak, Gayatri Chakravorty. "Can the Subaltern Speak?" *Colonial Discourse and Post-Colonial Theory: A Reader.* Ed. Patrick Williams and Laura Chrisman. New York: Columbia UP, 1994. 66–111.

———. *A Critique of Postcolonial Reason: Toward a History of the Vanishing Present.* Cambridge: Harvard UP, 1999.

———. "Subaltern Studies: Deconstructing Historiography." *The Spivak Reader.* Ed. Donna Landry and Gerald MacLean. New York: Routledge, 1996.

Stuckey, Elspeth J. *The Violence of Literacy.* Portsmouth, NH: Boynton/Cook, 1991.

Therborn, Göran. *The Ideology of Power and the Power of Ideology.* New York: Verso, 1999 (1980).

Trimbur, John. "Agency and the Death of the Author: A Partial Defense of Modernism." *JAC* 20 (2000): 283–98.

Ulmer, Gregory L. *Applied Grammatology: Post(e)-Pedagogy from Jacques Derrida to Joseph Beuys*. Baltimore: Johns Hopkins UP, 1985.

———. *Heuretics: The Logic of Invention*. Baltimore: Johns Hopkins UP, 1994.

Valesio, Paolo. *Novantiqua: Rhetorics as a Contemporary Theory*. Bloomington: Indiana UP, 1980.

Villanueva, Victor, Jr. *Bootstraps: From an American Academic of Color*. Urbana: NCTE, 1993.

Vitanza, Victor. "Critical Sub/Versions of the History of Philosophical Rhetoric." *Rhetoric Review* 6 (1987): 41–66.

———. "Three Countertheses: Or, A Critical In(ter)vention into Composition Theories and Pedagogies." Harkin and Schilb 139–72.

Whitson, Steve, and John Poulakos. "Nietzsche and the Aesthetics of Rhetoric." *Quarterly Journal of Speech* 79 (1993): 131–45.

Worsham, Lynn. "Critical Interference and the Postmodern Turn in Composition Studies: An Agenda for Theory." *Composition Forum* 10 (1999): 1–15.

———. "On the Rhetoric of Theory in the Discipline of Writing: A Comment and a Proposal." *JAC* 19 (1999): 389–409.

———. "Writing against Writing: The Predicament of *Ecriture FÈminine* in Composition Studies." Harkin and Schilb 82–104.

Žižek, Slavoj. *The Sublime Object of Ideology*. New York: Verso, 1989.

Index